Pr

"**WOW**...A must-read for all leaders, executives, and entrepreneurs. Mike does a phenomenal job of exposing the toxicity of limiting beliefs and negative thoughts as he moves us into empowerment. As I read *The Imposter In Charge,* I felt myself experiencing mental shifts. This is an incredible read for all."

Stacey O'Byrne, International Speaker/Trainer,
Author of *Secrets To Becoming A Master Networker*
and Success Strategist

"I've known Mike for the past several years and have witnessed his transformation from being overweight and lacking confidence to super fit and in control of his life. I can feel people's energy levels, and over a several month period, I noticed Mike's energy shooting up. One day we were having breakfast and his energy was so high that I experienced peace and joy just being in his presence. That day I hired him to be my business and life coach."

Bryan Schroeder, Owner
FasterHouse, LLC

"Mike Kitko is a top-notch human being with world class coaching abilities and real-world insights. I've personally seen the changes in the lives of many people he's worked with.

When I first met Mike years ago, I could see that he was a high-caliber business manager with advanced experience in personnel development and strong business processes. He is a strong leader, a sober sounding board, and a thought-provoker who inspires people to become better versions of themselves.

This book contains dozens of valuable nuggets that you'll be able to implement quickly, and it will offer you new insights each time you read it."

Art Snarzyk, Principal
Innerview Advisors, Inc.
"The Turnover Terminator"

"I hired Mike as my coach a few months after I started my franchise business to help me stabilize my emotions and anxiety while riding the entrepreneurial roller coaster. His coaching quickly expanded to my health, personal power, vision, relationships, business strategies, and more.

Through a varied approach that ranged from spiritual and emotional growth to mental clarity and executive business coaching, Mike got to the core of a multitude of issues with which I was struggling. Mike's honesty, level of care, passion, and ability to problem-solve are remarkable.

After completing Mike's coaching term, I can honestly say I'm a completely different person in terms of how I approach my daily life and long-term vision. I'm happier than ever and am focused on the journey, not just the results."

"With Mike's help, I was able to change my inner world, which had a direct effect on my outer world. The relationship with my family, my business results and, of course, my own happiness, have all grown through my work with Mike Kitko!"

Jordan Black, Franchise Owner
Two Maids & A Mop of Chesterfield

"Mike Kitko has a unique ability to guide his clients and readers on a journey to dismantle the limiting beliefs and behaviors they've developed and reclaim their true purpose and design for this life. Our work together taught me the value of being exactly me. Mike shifted my focus away from chasing external validation and led me "inside" to become a more fully realized version of myself. If you want to release shame, create more joy, or learn how to show up in a more powerful and authentic way, then this is the book for you."

Andrew Jasper, Owner
Jasper Agency - Farmers Insurance

"An amazing and incredible story of Mike Kitko's life journey, which led him to powerfully serve others each and every day. He now spreads those life lessons throughout the world and helps others move past their limitations. His story will inspire change for you too!"

Michael J. Sluhan, Principal
Genex Consulting

"*The Imposter in Charge* is a fantastic piece of work that's a window into a part of ourselves that many of us work hard to avoid. Slowly and quietly, the book reveals tools and insights that pertain to everyone. Through reading this book, I discovered that the man in the window is in fact me. One of the best books I've read in years."

John Burns, John Maxwell Certified Coach
Principal, New Heights 360 podcast

THE
IMPOSTER
IN
CHARGE.

MIKE KITKO

THE IMPOSTER IN CHARGE.

MIKE KITKO

Stonebrook Publishing
Saint Louis, Missouri

A STONEBROOK PUBLISHING BOOK
Copyright © 2019 by Michael Shawn Kitko
This book was guided in development and
edited by Nancy L. Erickson, The Book Professor®
TheBookProfessor.com

Library of Congress Control Number: 2019939991

ISBN: 978-1-7339958-0-1

www.stonebrookpublishing.net

PRINTED IN THE UNITED STATES OF AMERICA

10   9   8   7   6   5   4   3   2   1

DEDICATION

This book is dedicated to my three main ladies, the most important gifts I've ever received—Angie, Katie, and Meagan.

Angie, because of you, I was broken down and built back up as I was designed to be, not who I thought I had to be. Because of you, I'm the most powerful and loving version of myself. You make me show up when I don't want to. You make me step into the divine masculine I was created to express. You're my strength, safety, and comfort in any storm. We agreed to this journey long before we met, and there will be many more journeys together after this one. You and me. Me and you. Always. I love you with my entire soul.

Katie, the first time I set eyes on you was the most magical experience of my life. I'll never forget the moment I realized what true, unconditional love feels like, and the second you were born, I knew that feeling. I love you to the edge of the esrevinu and back, infinite times. If I had it to do over again, it would always be a beautiful day outside, no matter how hard it was raining. Maybe we'll get that chance again. Make others rise to your level of magnificence; shrink to no one. The world is better because of your strength and presence. You'll always be my right butt-cheek. Forever.

Meagan, when you were a baby, we knew you were special. You're intelligent, creative, analytical, thoughtful, considerate, kind, loving, and playful all at the same time. You light up a room with your laughter and amazing presence. Whenever I was down, I could always count on you to beat me at chess, take all my cards when we played *War*, or play any other game until you beat me. Your birth was premature, but that's because the world was ready for your magnificence. The world is better because of your love and leadership. You'll always be my left butt-cheek. Forever.

I've also had countless guides, mentors, teachers, and healers. You know who you are. I honor each of you for your contribution to my life and to the experience I get to embrace. You are each playing a leading role in this universal game we play. I love and honor you all.

CONTENTS

You're Never A Victim.

The first breath you ever took was an inhale.
The last breath you take will be an exhale.
These are involuntary and happen automatically for you.
You can't control your first or last breath.
What you do in between...
The happiness you create...
The relationships you discover...
The health you establish...
The wealth you build...
The love you feel and share...
Are all decisions.
They are all created by you.
You own your circumstances, outcomes, and direction.
You have full ownership, responsibility, and creative
    authority over them all.
The first step is complete and absolute accountability.
You're NEVER a victim.

INTRODUCTION

Before I rebuilt my life, I chased happiness, peace, comfort, and love outside of myself. The next promotion, salary increase, vacation, car, house, or material possession would cure all the pain, suffering, doubt, fear, and darkness embedded in every neglected cell in my body, in my chaotic mind, and in my uncontrolled emotions.

I thought the next accomplishment would make me feel validated, verified, capable, credible, and adequate.

From a young age, I sought confirmation that I was somebody. After years of abuse, neglect, and torment, I wanted to feel valuable. So I spent my life chasing wealth, titles, houses, cars, vacations, and external status.

I chased because I didn't feel worthy and valuable. I never possessed confidence, courage, and clarity of purpose or felt that I could show up as myself, which led me down a path of pain that caused me so much destruction that I was forced to rebuild.

I felt like an imposter in every leadership position I held. The imposter in charge. This caused my eventual collapse, like a self-fulfilling prophecy. I failed and needed to rebuild my life from the ground up.

The rebuild exceeded every expectation I could ever imagine.

I thought I had a good childhood. Some parts were good, but other parts contained traumas that required discovery and resolution. I was the chubby kid who was athletic enough to be picked for a team but was fat enough to humiliate in school and on the playground. I didn't have many friends, and those friends cast me aside when their other friends came along. My closest friend was another kid who didn't have anyone else to hang out with either.

I gained a lot of weight and had no girlfriend, true friends, or social life. When I was seventeen, I made some changes and lost about sixty pounds in three months on a crash diet. That got me some friends, and soon after, a girlfriend. But I still felt alone.

I graduated high school in 1990 and joined the Marine Corps in 1992 in hopes of finding confidence, strength, and courage. I hoped the abuse and the pain would stop, even though the villain and the victim were both in my head. I was a good Marine and ahead of my peers. I was promoted to sergeant after around three years, fast by the standards of that time. I was effective in my duties and was decorated with a Navy Achievement Medal for performance. I never served in combat, so regardless of my achievements, I felt like I hadn't proved myself. I never felt like I deserved the title of "Marine."

Before they could figure out that I wasn't worth the rank of sergeant, I exited the Marine Corps in 1997, and I accepted a position as an electronics technician in a Fortune 500 company. Over the next thirteen years with Tektronix and after a cross-country move, I had a management role and had earned a company-sponsored MBA. I was recognized as a high-potential candidate for a future executive role.

The label of "High-Pot" was scary to me because I was afraid that my leaders would figure out that I wasn't very good at my role. I survived a downturn cut in 2007 that shrunk my management team from seven to two. I had survived because of my effectiveness and abilities, but despite that, I feared they would figure out I was inadequate and fire me.

In 2010, I fielded a recruiter's call from Stanley Black & Decker and soon accepted a plant manager role, responsible for a $65 million plant. I was thirty-seven and held the keys to an organization I could've never imagined. Over the next three years,

I led a team that increased performance in every key dimension, including safety, quality, delivery, inventory, cost, and sales.

The operations team I built was the best in the business, and I'd measure them against any other operations team in the world. We could overcome any challenge. We were best-in-class in all of Stanley Black & Decker for working capital turns, an important measurement for the health of a manufacturing plant. We were powerful. I participated as an Executive Level Leader in the smallest division in the company but worked with a leadership team that established the vision and strategic direction. We had fun and grew the division to company-best performance.

After three years, I figured it was time to move on. It was only a matter of time before the gig was up, and they discovered I was a fraud. Even though the plant I ran was a top performer, I didn't feel it was due to my leadership. I ran again.

I was recruited by an energy company, SunCoke Energy in Illinois, and named as operations manager, the second in command of a $350 million plant. Again, I was an executive level member of the plant and the company. The operations manager was considered to be the heir-apparent to the general manager position. I intended to survive in the OM role, get promoted to GM, and build a world-class team as I had at Stanley Black & Decker.

I'd grown up in high-tech and light industrial manufacturing, but heavy industrial manufacturing was a new world for me. It was a difficult transition, and this increased my fear tenfold. Because of my fear, I showed up with bravado and outer strength I didn't possess. It was a facade. I was lost in the processes, how to lead my three teams of eighty people, and how to maintain or improve performance. I showed outer strength, optimism, and hope as I deteriorated on the inside.

So I could increase my personal performance, I was assigned an executive coach, and I survived the process. I was told that the company considered me to be the general manager-in-waiting, driven by my humility and development. I worked hard to show a stronger aptitude, but inside, I played survivor until I could be promoted and build a leadership team to protect me.

Promotion day never came. On a regular Friday in August of 2014, the GM pulled me into his office and fired me. For the first time since high school, I was unemployed. I got a severance, a few hugs and handshakes, and was sent home.

On the drive home, my head swirled, my mind raced, and anxiety skyrocketed. I was near tears. I walked into my house at around 11:00 a.m.

My wife, Angie, was at the kitchen table and asked, "Why are you home?"

"I got fired," I said.

She replied, "Oh my God! Wow." She looked at her watch, saw the time, and said, "We can make happy hour!"

And we did. We went to one of our favorite bars in the area where happy hour started at noon. We drank as many beers as we could before we picked up our girls from the bus stop.

I was consumed by shame and wanted to hide rather than face my daughters. I walked to the corner, and after a few minutes, the brakes squealed as the bus slowed to a stop.

"Dad!" my girls screamed as they got off the bus. They ran to give me a hug. "What are you doing home?" They were excited and surprised. That excitement made me feel worse.

"Girls, I've got some bad news."

Meagan, who was nine years old, looked at me with tears in her eyes and said, "Did you get fired?"

"I did, but we'll be okay, I promise," I replied.

Katie, eleven years old and with anxiety issues caused by years of trauma in our home, went into a panic. With tears in her eyes, she asked, "Are we going to lose the house? Are we going to have to move?"

My girls had hated it when we moved from Portland, Oregon to Saint Louis in 2013, but once they got settled, they loved our new home, their friends, and their new school. They knew that our lifestyle was now in jeopardy.

My severance package was generous, and it kept our finances in order while Angie and I hit happy hour four to five days a week, then picked our kids up from the bus stop intoxicated. Sharing time together with chemicals was what bonded our marriage.

I searched for a job about two to three hours a day before we hit the bars and even went on a few interviews. I was the runner-up a few times, and in the sixth month, I found another executive position as the general manager of a small firearms component manufacturing company in Saint Louis.

The entire fifteen months I was responsible for the firearms plant, I was in active alcoholism and worked hungover many days. Like I did at the energy company, I showed false strength and bravado, while I shrank to my strong manager, the president of the company. He demanded performance, and with all of my marriage and family problems, I couldn't commit my full attention to a demanding position and his expectations.

I was now a three-hundred-pound alcoholic with failing health and a train-wreck of a marriage. I physically, mentally, and emotionally abused my kids and wasn't capable or adequate to lead a company or a team. On March 18, 2016, I was fired again.

On the drive home, I opened the car windows so that I could breathe. The air was a brisk fifty degrees, and the smell of spring was in the air, but I felt like I was a character in a dream. The thirty-minute drive home felt like two hours, and during that time, I reflected on how all this had happened. I replayed the past two years over and over in my head. I was angry at myself, and my mind was in chaos. I tried to figure out how to avoid the pain of being a disappointment to my family. Again.

I walked in through the garage door. Just like last time, Angie was at the kitchen table. I was surprised to see that my daughter

I was now a three-hundred-pound alcoholic with failing health and a train-wreck of a marriage.

Katie, now fourteen, was home. She suffered from extreme anxiety and at times, stayed home from school.

"Did you get fired again?" Katie asked.

Slumping my shoulders in disgust, I said, "I did." I tried to be as calm, strong, and confident as a broken man could appear.

"Dad, how could this happen again?" Katie asked, her own shoulders slumped to mirror mine. My first-born was disappointed with her dad. I couldn't take my eyes off her, and I honestly forgot that Angie was in the room.

In an excited voice, Angie said, "Hey! We can hit happy hour!"

A few hours later, I met Meagan at the bus stop. I saw the tears in her eyes before she even got off the bus.

In less than two years, I'd been fired twice from two significant six-figure positions, and my bright future and executive runway were over. My resume looked like swiss cheese, and I felt unemployable.

We looked good on the outside. We owned a beautiful house and nice cars and had accumulated substantial savings. We'd vacationed so much that our girls had their own passports and had flown out of the country nine times. On the outside, we were living the dream, but inside our home, we were in toxic chaos.

I was suicidal. The things I valued were my income and title, and they were gone again. It felt like I had nothing and realized that I had to make some changes. On April 1, 2016, I began healthy physical habits. On April 7, 2016, I took my last drink of alcohol. By the end of April, I had hired a life coach. I adopted a new lifestyle, habits, and perspectives, which created an additional disconnect in my marriage. As I rebounded physically, mentally, and emotionally, my wife remained in active addiction and attacked my new choices. In June, I filed for divorce.

As I improved, Angie's attacks increased. In June, I met with a lawyer to begin the process of divorce. I wrote a big check and retained the law firm's services, which amplified my pain, fear, and uncertainty.

Back at home, Angie was upstairs on the phone with a friend. "Please get off of the phone," I said. "I need to talk to you."

"Wait a minute," she answered with dismissive frustration.

"It's important and urgent," I said.

A few minutes later, Angie, intoxicated from a cocktail of pharmaceuticals and alcohol, walked from the dark of the hallway into the light of the spare bedroom where I'd been sleeping for months.

"I filed for divorce today," I said.

"No you didn't," she said and laughed.

"I did. You'll be served papers in two to three days," I said.

Angie left my bedroom, disappeared back into the dark hallway, and went back into the master bedroom where she slept. I heard her get back on the phone and laugh to a friend that I'd filed for divorce. She didn't believe me. It was routine for both of us to threaten each other with anything imaginable.

The next morning, I watched the news in our spacious family room and searched for jobs on my laptop. At 8:00 a.m., Angie came downstairs with tears rolling down her cheeks.

"Did you file for divorce?" she mumbled through tears.

"I did," I answered with clarity, strength, and confidence.

"I don't want to divorce. I'll do anything!" she said.

At first, I resisted Angie's pleas for another chance. Over the next three to four hours, we discussed the past seventeen years. We reflected on the highs and the lows and then focused on the trauma and pain of the past two to three years. Maybe it was because we touched on some happy memories, but after hearing her ask for forgiveness and another chance with every ounce of ownership and accountability, we agreed to begin Narcotics Anonymous together that night.

In that discussion, we each asked for forgiveness and accepted responsibility for all the pain our actions and decisions caused the family. We started the journey that led us to where we are now. We've experienced relapse and struggles, but we're better because of my decision to file for divorce. Everything changed that day.

———

Today, I wake up at 4:30 a.m. every day. I carry out an intentional morning, a routine that builds incredible personal power, momentum, enthusiasm, confidence, and purpose. I perform breathing exercises to connect to my body and my breath. I meditate. Instead of avoiding emotion, I intentionally feel a range of emotions and connect to my humanity. I listen to audiobooks or read to connect to new knowledge. I journal to anchor this knowledge into my body because knowledge only becomes wisdom with integration. I do some form of exercise to keep energy moving in my body and to strengthen myself physically.

When my daughters, Katie and Meagan, wake up, I'm in my full power, ready to provide the love, encouragement, and support they deserve. I affirm them and make sure they understand how important they are in my life.

After they leave for school, I turn my attention to Angie. I'm present with her. We have coffee. We reconnect. I affirm her and show her that she's important in my life. We discuss family topics. We discuss our coaching business. We discuss household topics. We plan our day and sync up schedules. We're in control of our lives.

Whenever the girls are home, we have dinner as a family. I reconnect with them each night, listen to their day, and again affirm their importance in my life. I once lived to work. I no longer work. Instead, I give my talents and gifts to the world on my terms and my schedule. My family comes first.

Through my new life and business as a certified executive coach, leadership advisor, and speaker, in my first full year in business for myself, I exceeded my highest executive salary I earned in corporate America. Every day, I connect with hundreds of people through messages and videos. I light souls on fire. People are drawn to my message of life reinvention, and when they need hope, inspiration, and an example of possibility—I deliver. It fuels and energizes me and energizes others. Giving everything I have each day is both draining and fulfilling.

At the end of the day, I'm exhausted, and I've left everything I have in the world. I'm asleep by 9:30 p.m. My physical, mental, and emotional energy has been spent engaged and invested in activities I enjoy that are fun and entertaining. If I don't enjoy it, I don't do it. I refuse to live a life of sacrifice or pain or out of alignment with my values, vision, and mission. I lived out of alignment for forty-three years, and I refuse to live another day like that. I no longer feel like an imposter.

I spend every day in service to those who need my talents, gifts, time, and energy. However, I do this from a place of power, not a place of sacrifice. I learned from my mistakes. I suffered so that I could learn what I needed to learn, to teach others before they hit rock bottom.

In this book, I share stories and help you understand "the imposter syndrome" as well as strategies, stories, and actions that'll help you step into your power from where you are right now. When you're caught up in your own story, you tell yourself about your inadequacies or feelings of being an imposter, and you give others your basic rights and powers without resistance. You sacrifice yourself for others who you perceive as superior and worthy. You give away and grant others what you desire most: respect, dignity, and freedom. You give up more and more of your power over time. These are basic principles and concepts you concede, and when you take them back, you regain your power. When you regain your power, you regain confidence, courage, and clarity and take back even more of your basic rights and powers.

You can take back control of your life, your worth, and your value with shifts in beliefs and perspective and with a rebuild of your sense of significance. When you rebuild your confidence, courage, and clarity, you'll take back the power you've given up and will be committed and dedicated to your own happiness and well-being.

> **When you rebuild your confidence, courage, and clarity, you'll take back the power you've given up and will be committed and dedicated to your own happiness and well-being.**

Everything you read here might seem elementary. I believe that simple is best and that you cause the most pain to yourselves and your family when you overlook or refuse to understand and execute the basic and foundational things in life. If you will learn from my pain; connect with yourself; connect with those who are supportive and champion your success and happiness; and implement these basic elements, you'll move from a life of pain into a life of purpose. The journey can be magical. You'll realize that you're as important as everyone else but no more important than anyone. It begins when you put yourself first.

Introductory Work

Are You Showing Up For Yourself?

1. Do you feel that if you showed up in the world as yourself, you'd be rejected by everyone?

2. Do you feel like an imposter, a fraud, in how you're showing up on the outside compared to how you feel on the inside?

3. Do you feel like you're constantly on the brink of collapse?

4. Do you expect things to go favorably or unfavorably for you?

Try This!

1. Name all the people you feel comfortable being around and all the people that you're not comfortable around. List the common threads of each group.

2. When do you feel adequate? When do you feel inadequate? List the common threads in these scenarios.

3. Name three times when you expected failure and failure happened, and three times when you expected failure, but things turned out favorably. List the common threads in each group of scenarios.

Daddy Needs A Beer.

"Daddy needs a beer!"

When I said those words, my seven- and five-year-old
girls jumped out of my lap, ran to the refrigerator,
and raced each other to get me a beer.

It was fun. I couldn't wait to finish that beer so I could
see who won the next race.

That was a typical Saturday afternoon...

...and the fun had just started.

My little girls meant everything to me. They were always
in my lap.

In fact, I raised them in my recliner.

We were always together.

I was their hero.

They were either on my lap or right beside me.

They couldn't get close enough.

I call them both "butt" because they might as well have
each been one of my butt cheeks.

They were never away from me.

They loved me, and I loved them.

They were everything to me. The only light in a dark world.

Throughout a typical Saturday, we played games, watched
cartoons, they danced for me, they put on a show...

It was the best of times...

I never wanted it to end.

"Daddy needs a beer!"

And they raced to the refrigerator again, about to kill
each other to please their daddy.

They always pleased their daddy.

Until that certain point.

As they continued being perfect little beings full of love
and happiness...

I became a monster.

"Daddy needs a beer..."

And they hesitated to fetch another beer.

They'd seen it too many times.
In an instant, the same things that made daddy laugh
    and the same words, dancing, and laughter that made
    daddy fill up with joy...
Made daddy frustrated... angry...
Violent.
Screams. Punishment. Blame.
Things thrown across the room at his perfect angels.
They hated that daddy.
I hated that daddy.
The next morning I apologized, and the fun began again.
And since happy daddy was back, there was laughter,
    games, and love...
Until later that night
Then the monster was back.
As they grew older, after the first beer, they hid in their rooms.
I knew why.
I dismissed it as them growing up.
But they grew tired.
Their trust dissolved.
They'd seen it too many times and made changes to avoid
    the hurt and pain.
The pain that I caused them.
My beautiful girls.
It still hurts when I think about the pain I inflicted.
If I were granted one wish, I'd do it all again.
"Daddy needs a hug!"
And I'd cherish every race.
And I'd cause them no pain.
I love my butt cheeks.
Please forgive me for the pain I caused.
You were my greatest teachers.
You endured what you should never have had to endure.
And I now cherish every sober day with you.
You're my heroes.
And I appreciate every teenage giggle, laugh... and hug.

CHAPTER 1
PUT YOURSELF FIRST ALWAYS.

My father was a union steelworker. He came home after work, and my mom served dinner. When Dad sat down at the table, his responsibility ended. We lived in a 100-year-old, small, Baltimore row home; what's called a townhome in the rest of the country.

Our kitchen was ten-feet by fifteen-feet and was covered in brown and green 1970's-era wallpaper. The seams showed, the edges peeled and bubbled. We didn't own a dishwasher or a clothes dryer, and our washing machine was in the cramped kitchen. Mom hung laundry on outside clotheslines to air-dry our clothes.

"Babe, get me some milk," my dad asked my mom as he ate what she cooked and served him.

My dad's seat at the table was about four feet from the refrigerator, and mom's seat was three feet further than his. Mom dropped her fork, got up, walked to the refrigerator, and poured my dad a cup of milk. In our family hierarchy, it was dad first, the kids second, and mom was at the bottom. Mom's purpose was to sacrifice everything for everyone's well-being.

It was a strict, religious household, and I attended Catholic school until high school. Sacrifice was the primary message I received at home, at school, and in the German-Catholic neighborhood I grew up in. I was indoctrinated with the idea that doing things for yourself was a sin, and self-respect, self-care, or self-acceptance were reasons for punishment.

These poisonous beliefs taught me to sacrifice my own well-being. Sacrifice was never easy or fun, and it didn't make sense most of the time. We all had roles to play and a set hierarchy in the family, in the classroom, and on the playground. The higher you were on the hierarchy, the less sacrifice was required, and the more you could express yourself, but everyone preached sacrifice.

People who expressed their needs, wants, and desires were labeled as selfish and self-centered. Kids could be kids at Christmas and birthdays, and selfishness could be expressed at those accepted times, but overall, you only had that privilege if you were in a place of status or power. Because of this indoctrination, I shrank from my family, friends, coworkers, and leaders. I felt the pain of being unworthy and not valuable enough for my needs to matter, and I didn't feel adequate until my collapse decades later.

Leaders with imposter syndrome often sacrifice themselves and their well-being for the good of others and for the team. You'll allow—even force yourself—to become depleted for the good of the team.

The imposter syndrome causes you to feel less valuable and worthy and that you deserve less than others. Leaders with imposter syndrome often sacrifice themselves and their well-being for the good of others and for the team. You'll allow—even force yourself—to become depleted for the good of the team. Teams are as strong as the weakest link, and when you're depleted, or you live from a deficit, in time the neglect shows up in your results and the results of the team. When the leader gets better, the entire team gets even stronger. To heal, you need to recognize your own worth, practice radical self-care, and prioritize your own interests. Over time, the power you feel inside you will match your external power.

Recognize Your Worth

It was 8:00 a.m. on a chilly spring day, and Dad and I headed to the baseball fields for tryouts. It was an annual Saturday morning ritual. Still nearly asleep on the drive, I dreaded showing the coaches how much weight I'd gained and how I'd slowed over the winter. I'd failed to strength-train over the winter, as my dad had suggested. I was a failure, headed to the ball fields where an unfortunate coach would be forced to put me on his team because all the kids had to be picked.

I bombed the tryouts. It was awful. I struggled to hit, throw, run, or any other test they threw at me. I knew I'd receive a call the next Saturday from the coach who'd been forced to pick me. He'd call, and I'd pick up the phone. He'd tell me what team I played for and what position I'd likely play. The call came early.

"Hey, Mike. It's Mr. Gus."

"Hi, Mr. Gus."

"Mike, you're on the Giants. I'll be your coach for the season. I picked you first overall in the draft. Last year, my team needed a catcher. I need your arm and skills behind the plate. I'm counting on you," Mr. Gus said with a slight lisp and an older, crotchety, raspy voice.

"Thanks, Mr. Gus. I appreciate that," I said, stunned.

I thought Mr. Gus had made a mistake and confused me with another kid. That was the explanation for his kind call, and I was angry at myself for being such a disappointment.

I couldn't accept the fact that I had value. I believed that others were more talented, more important, and more valuable than me. Even when I was in positions of authority and responsibility, thoughts that others were better and worthier swirled inside my head.

As time went on and life came at me faster and faster, I dove deeper into my external challenges and didn't create adequate space to take care of the most important part of each of those challenges—me. It wasn't until I rebuilt myself that I realized the impact that neglecting my body had on my health, wealth, and the amount of love I felt.

I felt like an expendable commodity—valueless and worthless. And these feelings caused me to neglect myself further so that I disregarded my importance in any of the roles I served. I made life as difficult as I could for myself and dug a deeper and deeper hole each day.

Sometimes my feelings of inadequacy masqueraded as arrogance, ego, defensiveness, and aggressive behavior, but whether I was speaking with my leader, a follower, or a family member, I covered up the fact that I felt disposable. When I later reassessed what I'd learned, I realized that any need to sacrifice my well-being was a false belief, and that, when challenged, the belief collapsed under the test of truth.

Sometimes my feelings of inadequacy masqueraded as arrogance, ego, defensiveness, and aggressive behavior, but whether I was speaking with my leader, a follower, or a family member, I covered up the fact that I felt disposable.

The truth is that you were born with the same 99 percent composition of oxygen, carbon, hydrogen, calcium, nitrogen, and phosphorous as everyone else. You're made of the same elements found in the earth, stars, and universe as a whole. We're all born equal. There's no unworthy or worthless human being. Think about a newborn baby. Have you ever felt that a newborn wasn't valuable or worthy? Of course not.

When I realized that my belief that I was inferior or disposable wasn't rooted in truth, everything I'd learned about myself up to this point was open to examination. I explored why I thought I wasn't valuable. It was because I dismissed every accomplishment as being in the right place at the right time. Now I saw that wasn't true.

When I was a kid, every year I was selected for the Little League All-Star team because of my performance. I played trumpet in the school band and was selected to play in a "by invitation only" area band because of my talent. Because of my ability to learn, I was picked to attend the best magnet high school in Baltimore City. And because of my own merit and performance, I was promoted to corporal even though other Marines had been in the Marine Corps three times longer than me.

THE IMPOSTER IN CHARGE.

My military occupational specialty was 6492, Avionics Electronics Calibration Specialist. As a sergeant, I led a squad-sized (twelve to fifteen) team of technicians who ensured that the aircraft were mission-capable with accurate functionality. As a non-commissioned officer, I received regular fitness reports that assessed my performance and combat readiness.

"Gunny Griffin wants you," one of my junior Marines informed me.

I squared away my camouflage uniform, dusted off my boots, and made my way through the green interior of the mobile, deployable vans that smelled like mildew.

When I got to his office, I said, "Gunny, you called for me?"

"I did," said the salty, leathery Gunnery Sergeant Robert L. Griffin from Waco, Texas. "Let's review your fitness report. First, let me say you've done an outstanding job, Marine. Because of your leadership, military presence, and mission capability, you've been ranked the number one non-commissioned officer in the avionics division. That's shit-hot, Marine!"

Shocked and in disbelief, I replied, "Thanks, Gunny."

That's all I could choke out because I'd thought I was one step away from being deemed not equipped to lead.

Later, I was dubbed a high potential leader in two Fortune 500 companies, and my MBA was funded because of my high-pot designation. I assumed leadership for a $65 million manufacturing plant for Stanley Black & Decker at the age of thirty-seven, built a superstar team with the best talent I could find, and created the best working capital performance of any plant in the company. I was promoted many times above peers.

But I never felt good enough. I excused my accomplishments as being in the right place at the right time, and my internal chatter convinced me that "anyone could have done that."

I'd been taught that it was sinful to look for or embrace your strengths, talents, or accomplishments. A God-loving person measured their life by how much they gave of themselves for the benefit of others.

Let me tell you about fifth grade. Mrs. Anita Rostek was my amazing teacher. She's still my favorite teacher in the history of favorite teachers. That year, I nearly got straight As, and this was after I'd struggled and scraped by in my accelerated gifted and talented class the previous year. Fourth grade had been a grind from start to finish, and my father criticized me the entire year.

My first report card in fifth grade was all As and one B. I walked in the house excited and relieved, and I counted down the minutes. I was proud of myself and couldn't wait for my dad to get home so I could show him my grades. I was always trying to win his attention, praise, and love.

"What happened with this B?" Dad said, looking me straight in the eyes, totally serious.

"But look at the As, Dad," I said.

"I expect As, Mike. What do you plan to do about this B?" he pressured.

It was interactions like this that taught me that perfection was the goal. I believed that I was only as good as the thing not accomplished. Exceptional, but imperfect, the performance was average. So, I struggled to recognize my value and talents, which caused me to accept positions and roles while being blind to my strengths. I actually possessed exceptional talents but was numb to them. I believed that none of my achievements were worthwhile, and what I brought to the table was inadequate. I could recognize talent in others but could never recognize it in myself.

Three or four months after I started my improvement journey, I took inventory of all my accomplishments and the results I'd achieved. It was a remarkable list, and I saw that I'd been successful when I enjoyed what I was doing.

Then I shifted my attention to other people. I thought about every person I'd worked with and identified their strengths. I noticed what set them apart, made them valuable, and recognized their uniqueness that benefited the whole.

I realized that since I could take inventory for others and identify their gifts, and since I was made of the same collective stardust as everyone else, I also possessed talents that set me apart.

Those talents had created the successes I experienced. And since I could see strengths in others, it finally made sense that others could see strengths in me too. This was my epiphany; for the first time, I finally *knew* that I was talented.

Following my inventory of accomplishments, I listed the role I'd played in each instance and the qualities I'd demonstrated that brought about the results. I noted the qualities that showed up throughout: leadership; a relentless desire to absorb knowledge; the ability to spot talent and fit on a team; results orientation; the ability to motivate, inspire, and influence higher levels of achievement; and a commitment to constant growth.

I contacted a handful of people with whom I had worked and spent a great amount of time, and I asked them what they thought my strengths were. These were people I trusted and who valued truth over comfort.

"Rene, this is Mike," I said. "I need some help."

"What do you need?" he responded.

"This sounds strange, but I'm building a list of things I do well and the qualities you see in me. I need you to tell me my best qualities. I also need to know what needs improvement," I said.

"You're an energetic, enthusiastic, passionate, optimistic leader," he said. "You relate to and inspire others to achieve what they can and want to achieve. Your knowledge and wisdom set you apart, and you help others move into action and achieve what they thought was impossible. But you try to be all things to all people, and you're too hard on yourself."

Each person I contacted acknowledged that I'd made them better in our time together. That felt like home. It felt aligned with how I wanted to show up in the world, with the things that made me the happiest.

Most importantly, the things people mentioned as my strengths were effortless. They were the result of me simply being myself.

Most importantly, the things people mentioned as my strengths were effortless. They were the result of me simply being myself. What they said made me valuable felt like average skills to me because they came easy and were the things I do because I enjoy them, not because they were part of my job.

The same is true for you. The talents and skills that make you the most valuable to the world are innate. The things that make you valuable aren't what you sacrifice to do. They're already part of your design and are effortless. By being yourself, you contribute unique value and talents. You get paid to be you. When your talents are used to complement the talents of others, your true value is appreciated. When you focus on your weaknesses and what's left to do, it demoralizes and minimizes your true nature and value.

You don't have to sacrifice to achieve, and you don't have to do things you hate. When you move past a life of sacrifice and struggle to find happiness, you can make the decision never to do things you don't want to do. When you perform in your zone of genius, you create a lot of fun and enjoyment—once you get past the guilt of having an easy life.

And if something's outside your zone of genius, delegate it or hire it out. There's somebody out there who loves to do the things you hate. And don't worry about it being too expensive to hire someone. It will take them a lot less time to do the same task it took you hours to do.

Live within your own zone of genius. This is how you create maximum value for others, which in turn generates maximum value in time and income for yourself. Your value lies in what's effortless for you, that which you enjoy. Find what makes you unique and what you enjoy, stay in that lane, and watch as your life becomes more successful, free, and effortless.

Boundaries

It was well after 6:00 p.m., and I was nearing home after being at the office for over twelve hours. I smelled like the plant, an energy refinery that converted coal to metallurgical coke, which is mixed with pig iron to make steel. The smell of coal was embedded in my pores, and I saw the slight residue of powdered coal on my skin.

On the ride home, I decided that, even though I was tired, I'd exercise at home. I was done with the neglect. I was close to three hundred pounds and was disgusted at how I'd let myself slip.

I walked in the garage door, and my family was in the kitchen. Dinner was almost ready. I was hungry, but I decided to get in a fifteen-minute treadmill session before dinner.

"I'm gonna grab fifteen minutes on the treadmill," I said somewhat like a question.

"Dinner's almost ready," Angie replied.

"How long?" I asked.

"Fifteen to twenty minutes," she said, tension in her voice.

"Then I'm gonna hit the treadmill for fifteen to twenty minutes, and I'll be up for dinner," I fired back.

"Really, Mike?" she said. "Dinner is almost ready."

"And I'll be up in time. Call me when it's done, and I'll come right up," I assured her.

I changed clothes and began a slow jog on the treadmill. I listened to some heavy rock music to keep myself energized and motivated. I was on the treadmill for five minutes when Angie stormed down the basement stairs.

"You've been gone all day, and now you're going to take even more time away from the family?" Angie screamed at me.

"Is dinner done yet?" I asked.

In an irritated tone, she replied, "No, that's not the point. You've been gone all day. Now, you take even more time for yourself. Thanks for thinking only of yourself!"

"Angie, I want to get some quick exercise in. I'll be right up," I said.

"Thanks for all your help with dinner, Mike."

"Can I finish up my session?" I asked again.

"That's selfish, Mike, just like always!" Angie screamed.

"For fuck's sake, Angie! I'll get off the goddamned treadmill," I said with anger in every cell in my body as I gave in yet again to Angie's temper and lack of willingness to understand that I was committing slow suicide through neglect.

I was an overweight alcoholic in an emotionally, physically, mentally, and sometimes sexually abusive marriage. I wanted to be a great husband, a great father, be physically fit and free of alcohol, be mentally and emotionally strong and courageous, and get spiritually connected. I already felt guilt and shame when I put myself or my own needs first.

I knew deep down that each drink, each day without exercise or without proper nutrition, was sucking the life from me. I knew that I needed to make changes. I tried. I didn't always try hard, but I was trying.

"What do you think about us eating better, slowing down our drinking, and not going out as much?" I asked Angie.

"Then we'll have nothing in common," she said. "We might as well separate because the only time we connect is when we watch a game, drink beer, or grab a bite," she said.

I replied, "I didn't say stop; I said slow down. I'm tired of the way I feel."

"Selfish Mike again; it's always about you. Fine, but when we have nothing to do, remember whose idea it was to have nothing in common," Angie snapped back.

The guilt and shame I felt in childhood showed up often. When Angie said I was selfish, I felt the same emotions as I did as a child in religion class where I heard that self-love and self-appreciation were sins. Every time, I gave in to her because I feared her attacks; she attacked because she was in active addiction. She also attacked because I was doing something I'd never done before: I set boundaries. With her first challenge, any boundary that I'd established collapsed. I felt weak, which created even fewer boundaries.

I'm a morning person. I love to wake up before sunrise, drink my coffee, catch up on sports news, or enjoy my patio. My wife prefers late-night hours. I get tired between 8:00 p.m. and 9:00 p.m., and that's when her attacks heated up. Because of my body clock and sleep schedule, she threw words like "Old man" and "Grandpa" at me. Because I didn't want to deal with her attacks, I sacrificed what I wanted and succumbed to her pressure. I felt that peace and harmony in my marriage were more important than what made me healthy.

The irony is that I didn't experience peace or harmony or good health until I established firm boundaries that allowed me to practice radical self-care.

———

My first life coach's name is Paul. We began our friendship in 2007 when we sat next to each other on the first day in our MBA cohort, which we did almost every day after that for the next two years. Paul is also from Maryland, and we'd both moved to Portland, OR. Because of our connection and roots, we connected fast. When my family moved from Portland to Saint Louis in 2013, we maintained a connection, but our interactions weren't as intense or as frequent as when we both lived in Portland. I still spoke with Paul from time to time, and I followed him on social media.

"Own your day; own your life," Paul's Facebook post said.

Paul's belly overlapped his shorts, his shirt bulged out because of the pear shape he'd grown into over his forty years, and he posted a picture at the gym with him on a weight bench with a barbell in his hands. I laughed out loud because of the disparity between his message and the picture. Over time, Paul's belly shrunk, his waistline narrowed, and his pictures became more focused and intense.

"How you begin your day is how your day will unfold," his message read—showing a tight frame and muscle definition where there was once flab. The video that accompanied his post was of Paul navigating a circuit course with other cross-fitters. It was impressive as he climbed ropes, flipped tires, and carried sandbags for distance and speed.

When I began work with Paul, he talked about boundaries—a concept that seemed foreign, hurtful, and scary to me. I was sure that establishing boundaries in my marriage would be painful. I learned that when you begin to set boundaries after years of having none, it creates a shock to everyone involved, even when those boundaries are good for everyone.

On April 1, 2016, I stopped flipping channels on my television, got up from my recliner (exposing the worn-out head spot from years of wear), opened the basement door, and walked down the stairs. I set the treadmill for a half mile on slow speed, and I exercised for the first time in about three years. That single day started the momentum that propelled my entire transformation.

I finished the half-mile run. My chest heaved from the pressure of my inadequate inhales and exhales. Gasping for breath, I was covered in sweat. Self-judgment hit me hard as I attacked myself for my physical deterioration. I used to run six miles per day to keep myself in shape in the Marine Corps; now I'd let myself go to the point that a half-mile run was a struggle. I decided that, rather than berate myself, I'd establish a mindset that allowed me to maintain motivation for the next day, the next run, or the next workout. I also braced myself for backlash from my family.

"You know, we'd be better off if you'd look for a job instead of worrying about your weight," Angie attacked. "We need income, not your vanity."

I let Angie know that I wouldn't stop my physical exercise and that I was determined to get back into better shape. At the same time, I consumed lean protein, vegetables, and fruits.

"Now we're supposed to suffer because of your dietary restrictions?" she continued to attack.

I continued to cook all the same foods for the family that I'd always served, while I preserved my boundaries and ate what I chose.

On April 7, Angie and I were at an American Legion post, where we spent some time at the bar with other veterans. We'd joined the Legion as a means of building a network to find job opportunities. There were limited choices of beer. I enjoyed craft beer, but the selection at the Legion was awful. So, I had an awful beer to connect with my wife.

Right there, I made a decision at that bar over the sound of the Saint Louis Cardinals playing baseball. I finished my beer, and we left.

It was our common practice that I'd drive to the bar, and Angie would drive home because I was always inebriated. But not tonight. The radio was on, and I sat in the passenger seat of Angie's Jeep Wrangler.

"That was my last beer," I said,

"You're done?" she said in disbelief.

"I'm done," I said with complete confidence. My nervousness gave way to relief. I'd made my decision and set a boundary.

Of course, this didn't sit well with Angie. She was, after all, an addict herself, and she fought to keep her partner in addiction with her. Her attacks were relentless.

Over the next two months, I carried out rigorous self-care, and I didn't waiver, even in the heat of attack. I never tried to convince my family to adopt my new habits, and I didn't try to change the course of our family's behavior because of my new lifestyle. My kids watched my health improve but said that I'd made too many changes. Boundaries are like that; even if the boundaries don't cause others to make sacrifices themselves, people can feel shocked and become paralyzed.

Angie's drug use increased, and our communication halted. She planned trips without me and didn't tell me where she was going. Our marriage crumbled. She detached from the family and her attacks on my new lifestyle increased.

Paul was my valued coach through all of this. He taught me to practice a line that would create positive results. Whenever Angie threw an accusing insult at me, I responded, "You might be right; I might be a *blank*, but I love you anyway." Her most common attack was, "Mike, you're a selfish asshole." And my most common response became, "I might be a selfish asshole, but I love you anyway."

That response frustrated Angie, but it also defused the situations. She wanted me to attack back or relent, and I did neither. In the past, her attacks caused me to shut down. This time, I didn't waver. In June, I filed for divorce, which began the next chapter of our beautiful journey. Over the next years, we became two addicts who merged into a unified power-house marriage. The fact is that when one person gets better, everyone that person touches gets better as well.

Boundaries go beyond self-care. They must extend to who you allow in your life, how you allow others to treat you, what you give up for the sake of others, and how much you shift your own desires for the good of a person, a group, or an organization. No one else can decide what's healthy for you. They can make suggestions, observations, or recommendations, but no one has authority over you or can make decisions for you unless you grant them that power.

> **Executive leaders with imposter syndrome feel incapable and inadequate to establish boundaries that serve their interests.**

Executive leaders with imposter syndrome feel incapable and inadequate to establish boundaries that serve their interests. They become depleted over time and train others to expect substantial self-sacrifice, which brings on more pain. When you're emotionally healthy, you never sacrifice yourself. Healthy organizations never encourage their employees or leaders to sacrifice as part of standard expectations. Routine self-sacrifice drives you to fade over time. The more you fade, the less you can contribute. This process ends in disaster.

When you take back your power and set boundaries, others around you will meet you where you are, at your new level of self-appreciation.

Prioritize Your Own Interests

It was a hot and sticky midsummer Sunday evening in Baltimore. I knew I'd be without my dad for the upcoming week. With tears in my eyes, I sniffled and tried not to cry. We walked home from a fun day at the park where we'd played baseball and hung out.

"Dad, why do you have to go to work tomorrow?" I asked in a seven-year-old voice, sad that my best friend wasn't around as much as I wanted him to be.

"Because I've got to make sure you have everything you need," my dad said as we walked home with our bat, a ball, and two gloves.

"But I don't want you to go to work, Dad; I want you to stay home with me," I begged and tried to get him to quit his job to play ball with me full-time.

He replied, "But then we wouldn't be able to afford to live, Mike. I'd rather stay home too, but for us to have what we need, I need to go to work every day."

He told me that sacrifice was just part of life.

Later in life, I found out that life is supposed to be easy and fun. My dad loved me, but the lessons he taught me were that life is hard, earning money is hard, and sacrifice is required to get anything. I learned that "the man" was out to get you, and that if you're not careful, people will swindle and trick you out of everything you own.

My life was miserable when my beliefs aligned with those lies. Life *is* hard when you make it hard. But life is also fun when you approach every situation from a place of joy, love, and opportunity. When you look for the pain, you'll find it. When you look for the joy, you'll find that too.

I learned that I could squeeze the best out of my life when I prioritized my own interests. Interests and deepest desires are your compasses for happiness, and you'll stifle your creativity, energy, and joy when you stifle your interests and desires. If you suppress what you like and want, you're already dead. You're just waiting for your heart to stop beating while you pretend to live.

When I wanted to do anything that aligned with my purpose or interests, my family and friends challenged me. I felt like I was expected to sacrifice my time or fall in line with what other people had planned for me. I felt smothered.

For example, I felt an innate urge to become an entrepreneur. I didn't have fun or enjoy myself when I worked in corporate America. I didn't like the pressure and constant stress, and I didn't want to sacrifice for an organization that would replace me the second after I died from exhaustion or a heart attack. But I didn't have the confidence or courage to step out of the corporate world and take a chance on myself.

When I lost my jobs, I felt broken since my identity was wrapped around my titles and income. I felt like I'd lost it all. Of course, Angie expected me to look for a new job, so we could resume our lifestyle. So, I split my massive amount of free time between searching for a new position and creating a plan for a start-up business.

I knew our old lifestyle wouldn't make for a peaceful, happy family. We'd lived an unconscious life. I was employed and paid the bills, Angie did little for the family or herself, and the kids experienced two suffering and inadequate parents. But Angie expected to go back to that same lifestyle. It was all she knew and the only option she'd accept. Together, we were comfortable in our finances but miserable in everything else.

It seemed like the perfect time to launch a new life.

Over the next six months, I did a passive job search and went on some token interviews, but my heart was set on building a new business of my own.

———

I was soaked with sweat after a mid-day lift and run in my basement gym. I always gained tremendous confidence and clarity when I exercised. I walked up two flights of stairs and made my announcement.

"I'm going to start a coaching business," I told Angie as she was in bed for a mid-day, all-day nap.

"A what kind of business?" Angie replied with a skeptical smirk and holding back laughter.

"A coaching business. I'm going to help people improve their lives," I explained with confidence as the new vision for my life crept into my belief system.

Through her sleepy brain fog, Angie attacked. "We're going to lose everything because you can't find a job."

"No," I defended. "I'm not going back to work for another company. I'm starting a coaching business to help other people.

Not sure how yet, but the only thing I ever enjoyed in my corporate jobs was coaching people and building teams. I'm going to focus on that."

Since I'd first met Angie, this was the first major decision I'd made 100 percent on my own, for my own interests. I knew I'd have to enforce massive boundaries, employ courage, and resolve to make progress when I felt resistance from my family and friends.

When you've had the habit of walking the path that others designed for you, there will always be resistance. But stand firm in your truth. People will panic when you make a stand, but they'll grow with you once they become comfortable with the changes.

And so it began. That conversation was the catalyst for launching my new business. Angie hated the idea, but I started a business anyway. I finally did something that aligned with my values, desires, talents, and purpose.

This time, I forged ahead. I secured an LLC. I bought a URL. Designed a website. I networked. The entire time, I included those around me in everything and demonstrated progress.

I also went on about eight to ten interviews for other jobs, but I never wanted any of the positions. My passion was for my new business, and the universe stepped in to help me along—at just the right time, every time.

I was introduced to and met with James Brinkmann right when I was beginning to doubt myself. At the time, James was a partner in a real estate team, and we'd been introduced by another individual who thought we'd hit it off because we were both Marines. I was looking forward to meeting him.

We met at a café as the dinner rush was beginning, and the smells of charred meat and sautéed vegetables made my stomach growl. I didn't have any income yet, so I didn't spend on food outside of my house. I was still in a mental state of scarcity.

"Tell me about your team," I asked James. I was curious because I get excited by building high-performance teams, and I love to develop them to gel as a unit.

James replied, "I co-lead with two other functional leaders. One leads the buyer's agents, one leads the seller's agents, and

31

I build and develop the team. We have an admin, two buyers' agents, and we're looking for more agents."

I told him how much I enjoyed the team-building process. "What challenges do you have with your business and your team?" I asked so that I could understand his pain points and see if I could add value.

"I'm struggling to motivate them," James said in an optimistic, yet somewhat deflated tone. "We've got some talented people but motivating them has been a struggle," he admitted.

The walls were down, and we built some trust over a cup of coffee and our Marine brotherhood.

"What if I could help?" I asked. Those words flowed out of my mouth, almost by muscle memory, even though I'd never used them or practiced them.

"What would you do?" James responded.

An air of excitement built. Without hesitation, I said, "How about a workshop about high-performance people and high-performance teams?" The words came without effort. I'd never thought about leading any such session before.

"Sounds great. How long, and what's the price tag?" James asked as he braced himself, a look of apprehension on his face.

"Ninety minutes and $150. I'll also pitch my one-on-one coaching services." I leaned in for the response. I'd negotiated for other people and other companies before, but never for my own business, which at this point didn't even exist.

"Done. Let's schedule it," he answered.

By the end of the meeting, I committed to leading two ninety-minute workshops in one week at $150 each. I felt victorious.

From those workshops, I signed two private clients to coach one-on-one. Over the next three months, I signed four more clients, led three speaking engagements, and built a reputation for my ability to establish trust and engage in direct and honest relationships with my clients. Results soared as I helped them find their inner confidence, courage, and clarity. The idea of a job in corporate America was fully put to rest.

In my meeting with James, I'd made a snap decision that aligned with my values, desires, talents, and purpose. When we do things that make us happy, more happiness moves toward us. The law of attraction is real, without a doubt.

Happiness creates happiness. Excitement creates excitement. Energy creates energy.

Happiness, excitement, and energy create results.

Leaders need to lead. Your inner compass tells you which way you need to move. You must learn to trust your intuition. If you fight your inner compass, you'll live a life of regret and pain. Leaders who suffer from the imposter syndrome shrink and recede into the comfort of predictable patterns in and out of the corporate environment. When you gain clarity about what you want and learn to ignore the fears of others—including your family and friends—you'll take back your power, one decision at a time.

If you feel like an imposter, you've given up your own authority to make simple decisions in your business, life, and marriage. When you take these back, you'll grow in confidence, courage, and clarity about what you want.

> **If you feel like an imposter, you've given up your own authority to make simple decisions in your business, life, and marriage.**

When your professional and personal pursuits are aligned with your values, desires, talents, and purpose, the journey *is* the destination. Everything is possible and available to you. That's what happened for me, and you're just as capable.

Self-Care

I'm a Baltimore Ravens football fan. When asked how he found the time to fit a workout in every day, the team's old head coach, Brian Billick, replied that he didn't have enough time *not* to work out. He explained that there was so much to accomplish each day that if he didn't work out, he wouldn't have the energy he required to maintain his rigorous schedule. I'd heard this from him but ignored it for years. It didn't make sense to me; I was too immature to understand.

I'd learned I could use a variety of tools to create more space and time in my life, but the first major impact came when I implemented the concept of O.W.N.E.R., an acronym that one of my mentors used to describe the ingredients needed to attain powerful physical health.

"Once you integrate these activities in your life," he said, "your physical health will improve."

With intention and effort, the body heals and becomes more powerful and energized. Expansion and improvement in each area will drive continued growth. The five areas are:

O - Oxygen
W - Water
N - Nutrition
E - Energy/Exercise
R - Rest

Oxygen

The body needs oxygen to survive. When you don't get enough oxygen, you become depleted, and your breath becomes more shallow. Anxiety and panic then ensue, and your vital organs begin to struggle for survival. If you are getting too little oxygen, you can experience fatigue, depression, and lethargy. It's important to keep the oxygen flow cycling into your body. You can practice breath work or deep-breathing techniques a few times per day for one to two minutes to help your body get the oxygen it needs to promote peace, harmony, and calmness.

Water

Your body is over 85 percent water, and you lose water to exertion, evaporation, and the cleansing functions of our excretory system. When you don't drink enough water to hydrate, your cells are on the lookout for water, and the focus and attention of your body becomes survival rather than goal attainment. When you become dehydrated, you experience low energy and exhaustion, you crave excess salt and sugar, and you experience overall body inefficiency.

Nutrition

Food is fuel, not feelings. When you eat to sedate yourself, you risk weight volatility, toxicity, and improper fuel to manage the physical machine. When your nutrition is a source of fuel, and you ingest what serves to build and restore your energy, then you respect what proper nutrition brings to your lives—health.

We can overcomplicate nutrition, but it's simple if you select lean protein and fresh fruits and vegetables as your regular fuel. My family also incorporates high-quality all-in-one shakes with nutritional greens daily. Angie and I use shakes and they provide all of the nutrition that's been stripped out of the food available in most supermarkets.

Energy/Exercise

When busyness sets in, exercise can be the first activity we toss aside. Exercise builds energy, motivation, and stamina, and if we continue to increase the intensity of our physical activity, each of these dimensions will increase as well. We overcomplicate physical exercise, too.

If you don't exercise now, start with twenty minutes of movement such as light jogging, swimming, or basic yoga. I advise my clients to perform some form of exercise every day—even for only twenty minutes—to get their heart rate up. Increase intensity, frequency, and duration as your energy, strength, and stamina increase. The goal of each workout is to remain motivated for the next session.

Rest

Rest is the most difficult area to achieve for individuals who have developed a case of "the busies." If you create a pocket of eight hours without any devices, television, or work, your body will take the rest it needs. Some nights it might need six hours, other nights it might need eight. The most important factor in a good night's rest is to create your day around your pocket of rest, not rest around your day. Reduce your caffeine intake and set aside an hour to unwind or get frisky with your spouse, which will help your body take the rest it needs. This life is a marathon, not a sprint, so start where you are and improve the habits that create greater outcomes. Your rest will naturally increase as your deep breathing exercises, hydration, nutrition, and exercise improve and expand.

These simple steps are a great beginning; improve from there. Start small and increase the duration as your body develops. Begin with simple steps:

- Practice breathing exercises morning, noon, and night, or when you feel stress. Exhale slowly for ten seconds, inhale slowly for ten seconds, and hold your breath for ten seconds. This will flood your body with oxygen.

- Increase your water intake to one half of your body weight in ounces. (For example, if you weigh two hundred pounds, drink one hundred ounces of water.)

- Consume lean meats, fruits, and veggies.

- Minimize processed carbs and alcohol.

- Exercise for at least twenty minutes every day.

- Create a pocket for eight hours of rest without devices. Disconnect thirty to sixty minutes beforehand.

When starting off, don't over-exert yourself. Your goal is to keep your motivation high for the next day. With these simple steps, your weight will stabilize or begin to drop. Brain fog will clear, energy will increase, and productivity and motivation will improve. By following O.W.N.E.R. habits, you'll get more done in a single day because you have more energy. The sooner you implement these basic disciplines, the better.

Further, to enhance your mental clarity, do the following each day:

- Read or listen to material that expands your knowledge and mental capabilities.

- Journal about what you feel in your body, your emotions, your worries, concerns, and struggles.

- Journal about your wins and the critical tasks you need to accomplish that day.

- Meditate for twenty minutes every morning to increase mental clarity, mindfulness, and peace.

- Take one to three-minute "mind breaks" when you switch between activities during the day. Focus on your breathing and count your breaths.

After my crash, and before I started my journey, I didn't focus on my physical health. I wanted to make some money and go on another vacation—back to the comfortable life we knew. I had no idea that my physical health was a major reason I'd lost my income and, from there, my life spiraled. That's obvious to me now.

I didn't know that my breathing could impact my emotions. I drank little water, I ate whatever made me feel sedated, I hadn't exercised in three years, and I consumed large quantities of alcohol, which impacted my rest. As Jimmy Buffett sang, some people treat their body like a temple. I treated mine like a tent. I was forty-three years old, and when I look back at pictures of myself, I see that I was an overweight, worn out, unhappy man.

My family no longer attacks me for the changes I made. In fact, they allow me plenty of space, and they accept my self-care routine because that's what allowed me to take back ownership of my life, my health, and my ability to create wealth.

Meanwhile, Angie and the kids watched my reinvention, and Angie has adopted an intentional life as well. She meditates, exercises, and learns every day. Katie and Meagan have joined our health journey as well, and their nutritional and exercise choices have matured over time. Our marriage and family are stronger because I decided to set boundaries and refused to shrink when those boundaries were challenged.

If you're in an executive position of power, it's crucial for you to set aside time every morning and create a routine, so you can approach the day from a place of power. A powerful morning creates a powerful day. To feel powerful, you must own your day, your health, and your life—or they will own you. Practicing radical self-care and establishing healthy boundaries are essential to having personal power. A leader who suffers from the imposter syndrome might struggle feeling worthy of self-care and might ignore and neglect his or her physical, mental, and emotional work. The leader must take back power one day and one decision at a time.

As Jeff Olson states in his book, *The Slight Edge: Turning Simple Disciplines into Massive Success*, good habits are easy to do and easy not to do. You must implement and build the discipline it takes to remain consistent.

Chapter 1 Work

Are You Showing Up for Yourself?

1. What do you believe about putting yourself first? Do you believe that "putting your oxygen mask on first" is an act of service or an act of selfishness?

2. What boundaries do you have in place that you'll not flex, regardless of external pressure?

3. Are you easily persuaded to give up things that serve your best interest for the interests of others?

4. Do you feel powerful, worthy, and valuable just because you're breathing? Do you feel that your worth is conditional?

Try This!

1. List all the self-care activities you perform during the day. Hold yourself accountable for oxygen, water, nutrition, exercise, rest, and mental clarity practices. If you're lacking in any area, what's your plan to fill the gap?

2. Share your plan with your closest family and friends. Are they supportive? Are they encouraging and championing you to become the most powerful version of yourself? Your tribe matters. Make sure you only have people in your life who want the best for you and return the favor to all of those you love and support.

3. What passions and interests are you withholding from yourself? Why? Make a list of all of the things you'd love to do but aren't doing because of conflicting priorities. Make a plan to include these in your life, regardless of how much time you can devote to them. You deserve your desires and passions. It's time to get on with life!

My Own Prison.

I created my own prison.

Not the jail type of prison...

But the prison that I confined myself in was worrying
more about others' judgment than my own well-being.

I was guilty of this for many years.

I created my own prison.

I confined myself when I held back my words.

I confined myself when I shrank myself to meet others'
desires.

I confined myself by not showing up fully because others
didn't show up fully.

I confined myself by religion, theology, and beliefs that I didn't
believe but tried hard to adopt out of fear of judgment.

I confined myself by believing I couldn't be happy in
this life.

I desired more from life but remained confined out of
guilt and shame.

The thought of my own worthiness, value, and importance
created guilt and shame.

I felt insignificant because I forced myself to feel insignificant.

Those who were afraid to be themselves taught me that
I wasn't allowed to be myself, not allowed to live
happily, that self-sacrifice was the goal of life.

To seek happiness and fulfillment, to feel alive, to feel
free was a sin.

To feel worthy and deserving of seeking happiness, love,
success, fulfillment, joy...

Was shameful.

I believed that my mission in life was to sacrifice myself
and make others more important.

But I realized that if we all do that, we will all be
miserable together...

Are misery and sacrifice the purpose of life?

I reject that.

I believe that the purpose in life is to seek and find happiness.
Your own happiness...
In yourself...
Happiness is inside, and the absence of happiness means
    there's healing to be done to find that happiness.
It's in there.
Unbridled, absolute, unconditional love and happiness
    that has so much love to give to the world.
When you appreciate yourself, you have more to give.
You can love more.
Once you feel this love, you see the hurt, pain, and
    suffering that others live with...
You hear it in their words... their anger, their frustration,
    their pain...
You see it in their fatigue.
Suffering isn't the purpose of life.
Finding happiness is.
Not in wealth, materials, vacations, relationships, sex,
    chemicals...
But inside. In your connection to God and all things.
Suffering is unnecessary and not the goal.
To find the ease, the joy in life is...
It's there when you want it.
All you need to do is decide that there's more to life than
    the pain, suffering, and struggles you're experiencing.
The current challenge you're facing is temporary... it's
    not your identity.
Happiness is a choice.
Your choice.
It's all on the inside. There's no true, lasting happiness
    on the outside.
Every ounce of lasting, permanent, unconditional
    happiness and joy is within.
But you must be willing to release yourself from your
    own prison.
The prison you've created for yourself.

CHAPTER 2
SAY NO OFTEN.

The scene is a road in Mos Eisley. Stormtroopers surround the land speeder where Obi-Wan Kenobi, Luke Skywalker, C3P0, and R2D2 sit. The Stormtroopers search for the droids who have valuable information stored in memory.

"Let me see your identification," says the lead Stormtrooper to Luke Skywalker, dusty streets and the rock building in the background.

Obi-Wan looks at the Stormtrooper who made the request, uses Jedi mind-tricks, and says, "You don't need to see his identification."

"We don't need to see his identification," suggests the same Stormtrooper who made the request.

"These aren't the droids you're looking for," says Obi-Wan.

"These aren't the droids we're looking for," repeats the Stormtrooper as if it was his idea.

Nodding in Luke's direction, Obi-Wan says, "He can go about his business."

"You can go about your business," repeats the Stormtrooper.

Obi-Wan commands, "Move along."

The same Stormtrooper repeats, "Move along."

With this, the land speeder hovers away with grace.

———

The problem was, I had no spine. No backbone. I had no confidence to make and stick with a decision. Like that scene from *Star Wars*, I felt like everyone used Jedi mind tricks on me.

Frequently, I'd make a decision that was in my best interest or the best interest of those in my charge, and then I'd give in at the first sign of resistance or conflict. If there was room for challenge, I'd relent. In every area of my life, I struggled to balance my own needs and interests with those of my family or organization.

I'm now confident in my intelligence and ability to gain knowledge, integrate the new information into my life, and absorb it so that it becomes wisdom. I'm wise. But in the past, I didn't feel confident enough to stand up to a challenge. In circumstances where I was put on the spot to make a decision, I was good. I was grace under pressure. When there was time to consider all the variables, I was convinced without much effort. I didn't value myself, my worth, or my own opinion when I could be influenced.

When you feel like an imposter, saying no to anyone is difficult. You feel the fraudulence inside might be exposed. You're afraid that you'll be abandoned, rejected, or pushed aside. You think you don't have credibility, and any credibility that you do have, you concede without resistance. You remove yourself from the equation because of fear.

When you feel like an imposter, saying no to anyone is difficult. You feel the fraudulence inside might be exposed.

When you feel like an imposter, you must take back your power. Taking back your power requires you to say yes to only those things that serve your best interests, knowing that what's best for you will benefit everyone around you. You matter as much as anyone else, and you matter to those who really matter for you. Progress starts when you realize that you're not disposable, and when you recognize that your input and opinions are as important as what anyone else has to offer.

Realize You're Not Disposable

We're all equals. Sure, we might have different job titles, responsibilities, incomes, significance, etc., but we're all equals. The challenge is to feel as worthy as everyone else. It's easy to feel disposable when you're raised in chaos, pushed aside, told your opinion doesn't matter, or taught to be seen and not heard. It's easy to feel like an afterthought, like a nuisance in the way.

These feelings can cause lifelong trauma and pain. When you feel less than as a child, it's hard to bounce back to a place of equal value and worth. I was able to meet that challenge head on.

My dad arrived home after a long day at the steel mill. He sat at the kitchen table and read his newspaper after dinner. I saw that he was asleep, his body still upright, but his head bowed over, eyes closed, and dead asleep.

I hit the newspaper and yelled, "Wake up!"

He jumped, startled, and yelled back, "You son-of-a-gun!" It was his favorite reply; Dad never cursed.

"Can we play ball?" I asked with an innocent seven-year-old grin.

Even though he was dog tired, he stood up, and we grabbed the gloves and ball. He always said yes to the baby of the house.

When I was ten years old, my first niece was born. My father loved kids and gave extra attention to babies. He spent every moment of every hour that he was home with any baby in the house. When my niece was born, my parents agreed to babysit her almost every day, all day. She never left.

"Dad let's play ball," I asked on a weekend day. Mom was still home, and my niece was asleep in her crib.

Dad stopped whistling long enough to reply, "I can't, Mike; I'm babysitting Beth," and continued to read his newspaper. Frank Sinatra played on the record player.

"Mom's right in the other room, Dad. She can listen for her," I said.

Dad replied with some tension in his voice, "I'm babysitting Beth, Mike. Maybe later."

Later never came. I became non-existent. My father turned his full attention to Beth. I was the youngest of four boys in a blended family, and the only one who still lived at home. I sought attention, but it was impossible to find. Dad had always wanted a daughter. This was the first baby girl in the house, and he was attached. I became invisible.

After that, I struggled with abandonment issues all throughout my life. I feared that if I challenged people, I'd be abandoned. I even feared abandonment by those I disliked. I chased after people who harmed me. I didn't ever want to experience abandonment again.

This created challenges at home and at work. The greatest harm came in my marriage. My fear of abandonment created massive co-dependency. I didn't want to be alone, and I felt like I wasn't worthy or valuable enough to make a decision for my own benefit. Often, when I tried something to serve myself, I was challenged.

My fear of abandonment was too strong to ignore, so in most situations, I'd relent. Because Angie was a super-social creature, she would guilt and shame me into taking her out. When I did, we came home late, drunk, and the next morning, I headed to work with a hangover. It happened hundreds of times.

After I was fired the second time, Paul—my coach—told me to look at myself in my full body mirror in my bedroom.

"Say I love you," he insisted.

I couldn't do it. The words stuck in my throat. I hated myself. I hated who I was, who I'd become. I cried real tears. I couldn't choke out the words. I tried, but nothing.

After a few minutes of silence, Paul said, "Soon you'll look in the mirror with complete confidence, and you'll love and recognize how equal, worthy, and valuable you are."

I didn't believe him, but that was the vision. I didn't trust myself. I placed all of my trust in Paul.

Each day, I journaled and reflected on my life, and Paul helped me realize that I was a real human being. I, too, possessed a skin-suit, organs, and cells, and I breathed the same oxygen as everyone else. In meditation, I observed my thoughts, feelings, and emotions. They were real. When I exercised, I felt my pain. I wondered if I were more broken than everyone else.

We're all unique, but we're not different. It's easy to succumb to the doubts, fears, and chaos in our own minds. When you're unaware that everyone else on this planet has similar doubts and fears, challenges, and anxieties, you feel alone. We're all at war with our brains. Our brain's main function is to keep us alive. Stagnancy is our brain's primary way to keep us safe.

One day, as part of my morning routine, I recorded a reflective journal entry about my doubts, fears, and concerns. I then went into deep meditation, and I saw flashes from my career, childhood, and relationships through my mind's eye. The emotional movie reel that played was intense, and it was about the peers I worked with who also experienced self-doubt and fear. I saw bosses who made decisions out of fear and self-preservation. I replayed my mother's depression. I recalled my father's nervous breakdown. I relived my wife's trauma. I recalled my favorite spiritual teacher, Eckhart Tolle, describe the pain and depression he experienced through his life. I revisited my own pain.

I realized that no one experiences complete peace and calm. No one is always "put together." I wasn't broken, but I'd been holding onto childhood damage and trauma that caused me to live in a heightened state of doubt and fear. I could let go of the pain if I healed the abandonment trauma.

Carl Jung dubbed the part of our self that we hate our "shadow." My shadow included a boy who was easily cast aside and disposable. Shadow work allows you to feel the full emotional pain that trauma causes so you can begin to release it. To try to suppress, repress, or escape the pain actually keeps it trapped inside. Feeling the pain—all of it—allows the emotion to release and resolve. When the pain is resolved, you're set free from the doubt and fears caused by the trauma, but the experience and lessons you have learned remain. The trauma can then aid you the remainder of your life instead of creating fear and pain.

When you perform shadow work, you learn to accept and fall in love with things you once hated about yourself. You identify how the things that you hated served to help you in your life. The same things that make you laugh can make you cry. With shadow work, the same things that make you cry can make you laugh, and the pain becomes your purpose.

Your fear of abandonment turns into solid boundaries, and those boundaries attract those who accept your boundaries, your value, and your worth. Everyone has aspects they hate about themselves. And yet, those qualities can become your superpower when you accept the lessons and the beauty within them.

Now no one sets expectations or makes demands of me. I'm not subordinate to anyone. When my fear of abandonment creeps back in, I can recognize it and shift my mindset and heart-set. We live in a dynamic world where the metaphysical becomes magical when you recognize it.

Codependent people are bound and attracted to narcissists. Codependency is being dependent on someone else for life, happiness, and validation. Narcissists feed off of codependent people. When I didn't feel worthy or valuable, people who were ready to take advantage of my co-dependency were everywhere, and they found me.

When I allowed others to make decisions for me for my first forty-three years, I put myself second. When I didn't appreciate and respect myself, it was impossible for anyone else to appreciate me. Fact is, the world sees you as you see yourself.

Now I recognize my worth and value in this world where I once only felt pain. But because I've broken most of my neediness and dependence on others, I make my own decisions, form my own boundaries, and I stand up for myself where I'd once shrunk. It's become muscle memory. Once I formed and maintained healthy boundaries, people who respected those boundaries appeared in my life. I'm now surrounded by people who love me and who I can trust. As I developed self-worth, I found people who respected me enough not to challenge that worth.

You are not disposable; you're valuable beyond measure. You're ultimately accountable to no one, and no one has authority over you and your sovereignty as a human being. If there are people in your life who are abusive, make demands of you, or dismiss you, it's because you don't value yourself. Find your internal value, and people around you will respect you at that level of value. The world treats you at the level of significance you feel.

Change the inside, and the outside changes to mirror your inner world.

Your Opinion Is Important

"What's your approach to the handoff?" I asked with excitement because of my passion for leadership development.

"I want to document all the processes I use and hand them off to the team, so they have a jumping-off point," Bryan Schroeder responded with confidence.

"Do you trust your team?" I asked.

"I do," he said.

We'd been in his modest office for about an hour as we discussed his vision for the next four years. We talked about him handing off some of his responsibilities and authority that could reduce his team's dependence on him. Now, we discussed the tactical elements.

"Do any of your leaders know some of the processes?" I said.

"Sure, a good bit of them, but not all of them. When I'm gone, they execute in my absence," Bryan said, proud of his team.

"Would you consider asking them to document the processes they're familiar with first, to take some of the burden off you?" I said. I wanted to reduce their dependence on him sooner rather than later.

"Sounds like an option, but I think the handoff would be more effective if I gave them what I know." Bryan sat quietly for a few seconds.

"I can see how that might work," I said, "but that could also continue their dependency more than necessary. If we discuss the vision with them and let them know what's in the plan, they'll understand why they're being asked to document what they know.

This will help spread the work across the key stakeholders and leave you with only the work necessary for you to do."

"I see your point," Bryan said. "Both approaches will work, but I'd prefer to hand them the already completed processes."

To anchor the benefits versus the risks, I said, "How long will it take you to document the processes?"

"About three months," he said.

"What current work will you stop doing to fit that in to meet your timeline?" I asked.

He paused and gathered himself, "I guess it will take six to nine months if I squeeze in the project where I can."

"How urgent is this process?" I asked.

"Well, I'd hoped the handoff would happen much faster than in nine months," he confessed.

"How long would it take your team to document the processes that they know?" I narrowed in on the result that benefited him the most.

"They have the time since I do more than I need to," he admitted with a chuckle.

"Then we have an agreement?" I asked as I smiled and winked at him.

"The handoff starts now, I guess," Bryan said with a grin.

———

I evolved as a professional, husband, father, coach, mentor, speaker, and friend with each passing year. I noticed that my opinions were shifting as my awareness increased. My past opinions hadn't been wrong or unjustified; they were just un-evolved compared to now. As my world view and perspective shifted, so did my interpretation of reality. At first, this was difficult for me to grasp.

Because I felt less than adequate, I struggled to express and stick with my opinion. My low self-worth was a huge factor in not serving myself or others. Even though I had an opinion, I withheld it because I felt inadequate. I didn't realize that my opinion was, in fact, valuable.

———

I was in my office at Stanley Black & Decker when the CFO called me to his office. He was with my boss, Jim Kelly.

"We have to increase production to make up for some budgetary challenges we face. Can you run some additional overtime and work weekends to cover the gap?" the CFO said with a serious tone.

"How much do you need in total?" I questioned.

"As much as you can give us, Mike. We need all we can get," he shot back.

I looked for an opportunity to make up some ground with my production and increase capacity through my plant, even if that extra capacity came with a cost.

"Got it," I said in compliant agreement. "We'll run as much overtime this weekend as we can since it's short notice, and we'll run all-hands-on-deck overtime over the next few weeks," I said, a champion for the team.

I shared the situation and the challenge with my production leaders in my much smaller, less plush office off of the production floor.

"We'll run mandatory OT to get caught up and get ahead to help our division make up for some financial shortfalls in other operating companies," I said. I was a team player, and my support demonstrated this to my senior leaders. There were typical questions and even some whining.

"How long will we run like this?" one of my functional leaders asked.

"As long as it takes to meet our business objectives. We're agents of the company. We're here to meet our commitments," I said while staring each of the functional leaders in the eyes. I believed every word I said.

Mandatory OT went on for four weeks straight. We worked six mandatory days and offered the seventh day as a voluntary OT as well. My hourly employees saw dollar signs with the increased OT at a time when extra hours were scarce. Around the fourth week, I noticed my team's fatigue. They ran hard and were loyal. There were some normal grumblings, but overall, they worked six days, and most worked seven. I thought I could provide breakfast and lunch to keep them motivated and as a sign of appreciation.

I knew I needed to give them a break. I noticed the drag in their walk and body language. They didn't complain much, but they were spent. I was afraid to approach the CFO and Jim with my observation, so OT remained in full force. I heard the CFO's voice in my ears, "As much as you can give us." After the fifth week, my functional leaders told me the team needed a break. I knew they did, but I feared the confrontation with the CFO and Jim. I defended my position and told the team and functional leaders that OT rules remained in force.

After the sixth week, I was called into the CFO's office again. Jim was there too.

"Mike, give the guys a break. They're tired. Skip every other weekend and take away the seventh day as an option," Jim said with a compassionate tone.

"That's a great idea. I'll tell the team today," I replied, defeated because I knew it was right. I was disappointed that I didn't make the call myself.

I knew what was good for my team, but I lacked the fortitude and confidence to create a healthy situation. A senior leader made that decision for me even though that was my responsibility. I was humiliated and embarrassed. I knew better.

I expressed the plan to my functional leaders. I didn't take credit, but I didn't give credit either. I stated the plan as it was laid out for me. I was embarrassed, and I'm sure they saw through my words. It took more future failures and embarrassment to learn that my opinion was valuable.

————

"Why doesn't your opinion matter?" my coach, Paul, asked.

It never has, I thought to myself. With that question, I began to understand that my feelings of inadequacy had been fabricated in my own mind and emotions. My experiences, beliefs, and inner doubts formed unhealthy programs that made me feel inadequate to express my opinion, even though all evidence demonstrated that I was talented, worthy, and capable of a healthy opinion and point of view.

I had to work on this, so I began with small steps. I increased my awareness. I realized that I could express an opinion when I felt like the opinion couldn't be challenged, like when I expressed a personal preference or decision that wasn't fact-based. Those were easy—music, food, hobbies, entertainment, and other personal choices. I had no problem expressing my opinion about personal preferences.

But I felt inadequate when it came to opinions that were not personal, where another person could have a different perspective on the same thing. If I was challenged, I felt broken. I felt like I needed to be perfect and know all things all the time. If I had to say, "I don't know," I felt like a failure. If I didn't have an answer, I felt incompetent. I needed to be perfect, even when perfection was impossible.

I felt like an imposter when I might be wrong. I felt like an imposter when I didn't have infinite experience and when I hadn't been exposed to the infinite numbers of circumstances to prepare me for life's infinite possibilities.

A mentor helped me see myself as I saw myself. He said that my failure to feel perfect fueled my feelings of inadequacy.

"How has your inadequacy served you?" he asked me on a coaching call.

"It hasn't," I replied.

"You've never grown?" he countered.

I had healed a ton since I'd begun my journey, and I knew that he knew this.

"Guess what fueled that growth?" the mentor followed up.

Silent for a second, I paused for a moment. "Inadequacy!" I said in an a-ha manner.

"Exactly!" he said. "Most people want their inadequacies or insecurities to go away. But it's our insecurities and inadequacies that drive our growth. Without a sense of insecurity or inadequacy, we might all sit on the couch and rot. The inadequacy that you want to push away or fix is what drives you to grow. Honor it and use it to your advantage."

I finally understood that perfection is impossible, and my feelings of inadequacy drive growth. I felt like I could actually express an opinion at my current level of awareness that would benefit someone else at theirs, so I was free to share openly. He taught me that when I began with the words, "From my perspective" and ended with, "What am I missing?" I didn't have to be afraid of sharing my opinion.

With this technique, I could share my opinion and be humble enough to know perfection is impossible. I could ask for feedback on my current perspective instead of stating it as fact, which would open up a new way to expand my knowledge and wisdom. I didn't need to pretend to be perfect, and I didn't need to feel like an imposter. Now I could be satisfied as an imperfect and aggressive seeker of new wisdom.

When I'm coaching and teaching, I tell my audience. "You have something to teach me." There's never a one-way relationship; learning is always two ways. I seek to understand, and I approach every conversation as if I can learn, then when I realize I have something valuable to contribute, I begin with, "From my perspective" and end with, "Am I missing something?" When two people collaborate from a place of vulnerability, wearing no masks, the outcome is greater than when two people withhold from each other.

The imposter syndrome develops when you think that perfection is possible. When you accept that everyone is imperfectly perfect, the fear resolves.

The imposter syndrome develops when you think that perfection is possible. When you accept that everyone is imperfectly perfect, the fear resolves. Believe that your opinion matters, and even when you feel like an imposter, you'll take back the power you'd given up.

Chapter 2 Work

Are You Showing Up For Yourself?

1. Are you comfortable saying no when the other person's interests are in conflict?

2. Do you feel replaceable or disposable?

3. When you have an opinion, do you trust yourself to express it without fear of judgment?

4. Do you look for reasons to say yes or reasons to say no immediately after a question is asked?

Try This!

1. The next time someone asks your opinion on a pressing topic that isn't personal, take a deep breath and respond with, "In my experience..." and then provide your response. Complete your response with, "Am I missing anything?"

2. During your meditation session, bring yourself to feel the energy in your body. Bring to mind someone significant to you and recall a time when they might have held the same feeling in their body. Recognize that all humans experience every emotion. Recognize that you're unique, but not different.

3. Recall one experience in your life that you would rather forget. Journal the lessons you learned from that experience that were positive in nature and only about you. This might be difficult at first but recognize that every painful experience in life holds a lesson that can be a powerful benefit.

Shrinking.

The universe is a genius trickster.
I've heard that people "discover" themselves late in life.
I disagree.
We know who we are. We know how to succeed, how to be
　　happy, how to live the life of our dreams.
Newborns and toddlers have it all figured out.
When we were toddlers, we were loved abundantly and
　　received all we needed.
We got to be our natural selves, and we were happy and
　　successful.
Our true nature, our uniqueness, was our competitive
　　advantage.
But as we grew older, we were taught the "rules" of life.
Those around us showed us how to fit into life's box and
　　how the world operates.
Our parents taught us that we couldn't be ourselves and
　　succeed.
Our siblings taught us that we couldn't be ourselves and
　　succeed.
Our teachers taught us that we couldn't be ourselves and
　　succeed.
Our friends taught us that we couldn't be ourselves and
　　succeed.
Our bosses taught us that we couldn't be ourselves and
　　succeed.
We suppress ourselves, withhold ourselves, shrink
　　ourselves, thinking that is how to succeed in life.
We fall out of love with ourselves because we're never
　　good enough.
I'm not enough. I will never be enough.
You can't be yourself and succeed at this game of life...
We change our personality and how we show up to fit
　　into the world...
And never understand how to both succeed and be happy.

We ultimately choke ourselves, our true nature, and
    wonder why we can't find happiness.
Then one day, we realize what happened, and we begin to
    act like that toddler again...
We let ourselves rip, suppressing nothing.
And we find all the love we desire inside and out, along
    with earthly success and fulfillment.
We fall back in love with ourselves.
We use our uniqueness, our strengths, our gifts, our
    talents.
And find that the world has been starving for those things.
People needed us, but we never felt as though we could
    deliver.
Then we find joy, happiness, and love...
From being ourselves and delivering our true selves to
    the world.
The universe is a genius trickster...
And the greatest lesson you'll ever learn is that you're
    enough.
Right now.

CHAPTER 3
SHOW UP REAL.

Life happens fast, often at lightning speed. For years, I looked forward to the day when the next big thing happened or the current chapter closed. When I was in high school, I couldn't wait to graduate. When I was in the Marine Corps, I looked forward to separation day. During my time in corporate America, I looked forward to the next promotion, pay increase, or title. With each station in life, I looked forward to the next. I focused on the future. I never took the time to be present, to debrief on the past, or appreciate who I was at that current moment. I didn't appreciate who I was, so I always felt I was in over my head, and this made me feel like a fraud—an imposter.

My lack of presence led to a lot of unnecessary suffering and pain. Gaining radical self-awareness is the first step for you to gain the confidence, courage, and clarity it takes for aligned execution. Radical self-awareness means you have deep awareness, connection, and acceptance of your deepest truths, desires, vision, beliefs, emotions, feelings, thoughts, fears, strengths, talents, and weaknesses. Your self-awareness is so strong that you're able to make intuitive choices that support your healing, growth, and overall well-being.

Aligned execution happens when you operate in your strengths and talents, being unapologetically authentic and aligned with your true passion and purpose. Aligned execution is acting in a way that supports, promotes, and leverages your radical self-awareness.

Alignment is what allows you to appreciate your journey and any achievement. You become confident in yourself by acknowledging and embracing who you are and the challenges that supported you on your journey. You fall in love with your current level of awareness, strengths, talents, and even your current limitations. You embrace daily improvement out of love and not fear. You learn to embrace and trust yourself where you are, not where you think you should be. From that confidence, you begin to face the world as the authentic you.

When you feel like an imposter, you feel like you need to hide from others. You can't expose who you are because you're afraid that you're not enough—and not good enough—for whatever role you're in at the time. The imposter in charge feels the need to escape before being discovered as incompetent.

> When you feel like an imposter, you feel like you need to hide from others. You can't expose who you are because you're afraid that you're not enough–and not good enough–for whatever role you're in at the time.

To show up real, you can seek a neutral coach or mentor to gain radical self-awareness; ensure your talents and strengths are recognized, appreciated, and utilized in your role; and become honest with those around you about your key gifts that will allow you to be the most successful. When you know yourself at your core and fully embrace the true essence of the power within you, you'll face the world from a place of strength and opportunity.

Seek A Neutral Coach or Confidante

We all have blind spots. It's estimated that we operate from our subconscious over ninety-five percent of our life. When we operate from our subconscious, we walk, talk, and behave in ways we may not even realize. The most relatable example is when you drive to the grocery store or work and don't even remember how you got there. Your subconscious takes over, and your conscious mind wanders to the solve problems the conscious part of our brain creates.

Our hidden beliefs and behaviors reside in what's buried in our subconscious. Think about someone who sleepwalks. You can watch them, and when they wake up, you can tell them everything they did—and they'll be surprised about the experience and their actions. This is exactly how you operate for 95 percent of your life. Your subconscious programs shield your blind spots from your conscious awareness, and unless you ask others for feedback about your subconscious patterns, you might not understand your tendencies. Blind spots keep you stuck until your subconscious programs are brought to conscious awareness.

This is the role coaches and mentors play. They wake you up to the real you. There's no shame in having blind spots; we all have them. What might keep you from seeking and acknowledging your blind spots is the pain of fear, unhealthy pride, and ego. Successful professionals hire coaches. Amateurs pretend they can do better without a coach or try to go it alone—and they continue to underachieve.

One of my clients, Todd, came to me because he realized that he had blind spots. He was humble enough to seek help from a coach instead of staying stuck.

He needed someone he trusted who could recognize his blind spots and who could discuss his concerns, fears, and doubts. As a neutral party who doesn't feel the emotions of those doubts, it's easy for me to spot self-perceived limitations, upper limits, and blind spots. If you can drop your ego and allow someone else in, you can blow through your false limits.

"I'm looked at as the small accounts guy, and I haven't been able to break out of that role," Todd stated in our first phone conversation.

"What does that mean?" I asked.

"They give me all of the small customer accounts, and they hand my partner all the bigger accounts. I'm missing something. I know I have a blind spot; I just don't know what it is. I'm thinking of hiring a coach to help me understand how to break through."

"Do you know what an upper limit is?" I asked Todd.

His curiosity piqued, he replied, "Tell me more."

"Each of us has limits to the happiness and freedom we'll allow into our lives. When you run up against a plateau, you've reached a self-imposed upper limit, and it takes awareness and recognition to break through. I can help with that," I said.

There was a pause, and Todd said, "Interesting."

I learned that this was the word Todd used when he needed more time to process an idea.

I continued, "Our brains and our bodies seek comfort in the familiar, and when we begin to reach goals that put us in new, unfamiliar territory, we might self-sabotage to remain comfortable. It's a typical human response that keeps us stuck. The goal is to become aware of the upper limit and move beyond it."

I recommended a book by Gay Hendricks called *The Big Leap: Conquer Your Hidden Fear and Take Life to the Next Level.* It describes upper-limiting, how to recognize when you've reached your limit, and how to move beyond.

"I'm going to buy that book today. When can we meet to discuss coaching?" Todd asked.

Our first official coaching session helped Todd to feel normal. Years ago, I was introduced to Human Design, a personality system that enables heightened awareness of an individual's design, how to approach life in an aligned manner, and the key emotional challenges they face. The tool helps people feel normal in the ways they think, feel, emote, and experience the world.

I use a three-stage approach to help the client find alignment:

1. Remind them who they are in their design.

2. Reawaken their body, mind, and emotions.

3. Realign them with their true purpose in this human experience.

I launched Todd's program with an introduction to his Human Design profile. We were in my favorite coffee shop on Main Street in my current hometown of historic Saint Charles, Missouri. It was our normal meeting spot, and there was a lot of activity and the smell of fresh ground coffee beans, the sound of frothed milk, and the chatter of patrons all around us.

"Your design shows that you desire to show up as a principled leader. Your values and principles mean everything to you, and your ability to lead is your definition of success or failure. If you have no one to lead, you feel incomplete, and when you feel like you can't live by your principles and values, you feel incongruent and out of balance with your integrity—like a failure. Does that feel like truth?" I asked.

"Exactly," Todd replied in his usual reserved nature.

"And what I perceive is that your values and the values of those around you are not in alignment. You feel like you're forced to bend your principles, which creates an extreme conflict in you," I said as I analyzed his chart.

"That's incredible," Todd said after he inhaled, held his breath for a few seconds, and exhaled with a sense of validation.

"Why do you feel like you can't express your own values?" I asked.

"I'm not sure. Confidence? Sometimes I feel like I can't be myself since it might be perceived as being resistant to business growth," Todd admitted.

"I understand," I said. "Do you think that might be your blind spot? Do you think you're shrinking yourself and are coming across as unauthentic and underconfident, so management pours more into others who are aligned with their values and are authentic in how they show up?"

"That makes sense," he answered.

We both paused to sip our drinks and allow the new insights to soak in. It felt like we'd hit the nail on the head.

Todd and I worked together for a few months. His principles and ideals were solid. Nothing outside of him needed to change. It was his lack of self-awareness and self-acceptance that caused the resistance he felt from others.

Our conversations revolved around his current challenges; his beliefs about those challenges; the limitations he felt; and any options, approaches, or perspective adjustments we might consider. We uncovered his blind spots surrounding inadequacy, and I reminded Todd that he was worthy of feeling important, valuable, and showing up as himself. Sometimes, people need to get permission from someone else, even as adults.

We put steps in place for Todd to show up as himself in his professional meetings, without apology or conditions. The way he could recognize internal freedom and external success was to stand firm in his principled approach and uncompromising values, whether in his current company or otherwise. Sacrificing his principles and values to achieve results created cognitive dissonance for Todd. If he achieved any goal while operating in this manner, he felt unfulfilled. He didn't want that anymore.

"I've opened up more and more," Todd told me at a later session. "I'm more confident every time I say what I feel."

I dug deeper, "Has anyone shut you down? Has anyone taken away your seat at the table? Have you lost any business?"

"No," he said. "In fact, I set boundaries and don't take every low-end client anymore. I talked to my business partner, and he agrees that I can't keep scraping the bottom and meet my financial objectives. My bosses agree, too. I've opened up more and expressed myself," he said.

"How does that feel?" I asked, confident that he felt a new level of freedom.

"Feels great. I refuse to shrink for everyone's benefit. I'm stepping up," Todd said, satisfied.

Not long after, Todd was featured in a local trade magazine as one of the top new advisors in the area. He'd never felt worthy or powerful before because he'd never established enough self-awareness to realize that he could express himself. Now he felt his personal power that allowed him to show up as himself.

Todd is now confident when he communicates his perception of what's realistic. He approaches everything from his, the company's, and his client's best interests. He no longer sacrifices himself. He seeks out and expects support from his company and his peers, and he speaks up to realign expectations when necessary.

Professional leaders who suffer from imposter syndrome might feel that seeking support and help is a sign of weakness and failure. In fact, the opposite is true. The most successful individuals in the world have coaches, mentors, and sometimes an army of personal advisors. No one can do it alone. Everyone has blind spots and requires some level of support.

When you admit you need support or have blind spots, you can take back your power. You become stronger when you admit that you don't have it all figured out. People who think they've arrived are usually farther off-target than the imposters in charge.

> **Professionals who suffer from imposter syndrome might feel that seeking support and help is a sign of weakness and failure. In fact, the opposite is true.**

Align Your Strengths with Your Role

There are three basic categories in a skills inventory: strengths, non-strengths, and debilitating weaknesses. Strengths are those talents and gifts that were developed or were present from birth that you can rely on for success. They're effortless for you, and you get excited about performing them. In *The Big Leap: Conquer Your Hidden Fear and Take Life to the Next Level*, Gay Hendricks named this our "zone of genius." The longer you remain in your zone of genius, the more effortless life will be, and the more successful your outcomes.

Non-strengths are those skills that just get the job done with an adequate level of skill, haven't been sharpened, are not required, and that you can avoid and still be successful. Sometimes, you can delegate these skills to someone else who has them within their zone of genius. You can ignore your non-strengths with the right support. But if you focus on these areas, you reduce the potential for the powerful outcomes you can generate if you stay in your zone of genius. You'll never have time to sharpen every skill, nor do you need to.

Debilitating weaknesses are those skills you lack but must perform at a high level in your current roles. They can't be avoided or delegated. Examples of debilitating weaknesses are an engineer who isn't good at math, a leader who won't engage with people, or a figure skater who can't ice skate.

I inherited a quality manager who was promoted to a position that didn't suit him. We'll refer to him as Chad.

Chad and I took a walk through the quality area at the rear of the plant where shipments and deliveries were made. There were boxes scattered on the floor with outbound and inbound material. "What's happening with this box?" I asked with sincere curiosity.

"Let me check," Chad replied. "Hey, Jon, what's up with this box?"

Jon stood about ten feet away and was discussing another issue with his quality teammate, Gary. "Not sure, but I can find out for you. I'll be right out!" Jon yelled from the quality office. Chad and I stood on the noisy, darkened shop floor where the sound of mills, lathes, and grinders made it hard to hear.

It was near 11:00 a.m., and the morning delivery had been received. Boxes were strewn everywhere. The incoming and outgoing materials were mixed together, and paperwork stuck out from each box. "Jon will be right out to give us an update on the material in that box," Chad expressed with confidence.

A bit agitated, I said, "Chad, the quality department is the department responsible for defining sound processes. It's your job to define processes that don't require a person to pull a piece of paper out of a box that's mixed in with other boxes to understand if it's coming or going."

Chad looked confused. "This is how we've always done it, and it works."

"Which boxes did you receive today, and which ones are outbound?" I asked.

"Jon knows," Chad said.

"But you don't know. I don't know. Does Gary know?" I asked.

"Jon knows; that's his area," he said. The a-ha expression on his face told me he now understood my concern.

I took a deep breath and paused. "I need anyone on the floor to be able to understand the status of this material by looking at it. We need to know what's coming and what's going. I need us to know the raw material from the finished product. I need us to know the good material from the defective. We need to be able to see it without having Jon investigate. It needs to be obvious," I advised.

I overwhelmed Chad. These were basic manufacturing concepts. We were playing checkers, and I needed a team who played chess. I had set a goal to be the best plant in the division. If we were going to improve to that level, we needed to step up our game and be aggressive in every area.

When I'd assumed responsibility for the plant, Chad had already been the quality manager for three years. During that time, there'd been an increase in the number of field defects and internal test failures, which added costs to the plant. The quality manager is responsible for all quality metrics and the cost of testing, and our quality area was in chaos. It was obvious why our quality was substandard.

The entire area was a mess. Everything was jumbled together. There were few defined processes to determine the parts or assemblies to be tested; there were no specific areas to store the parts and assemblies that had passed or failed; we had few test procedures and no process flow charts to define the flow through the area. It was a nightmare.

It wasn't just the physical area that was disordered. Our monthly internal audits weren't being executed according to the plant's International Standards Organization (ISO) certification. Our last external audit had been months earlier, and it revealed some discrepancies that were still unresolved. When I spoke with the members of the quality department, they said these lapses were because they didn't have enough manpower, but I noticed that they were often on break or chatting with people they didn't support.

I knew there was a lot of work to do. First, I sought to understand Chad's responsibilities and authorities. It was clear that he'd been promoted into a role for which he wasn't experienced, educated, prepared, or equipped to lead. So I challenged him to lead.

I offered him ISO auditor certifications, quality training courses, and any classes that would support his growth. I set some lofty expectations for the new vision of the quality department and processes, and I wanted to invest in his development. I looked for some signs that he accepted my new level of expectations. I hoped he'd respond with a willingness to embrace growth. I wouldn't budge in this area; I demanded self-motivated growth from my leaders.

Chad and I had many uncomfortable conversations over the next few months, but he made no progress. It was time to make a decision. Either Chad would increase his skill set, or he'd be replaced.

I initiated the company's formal process for performance management. As we sat at a small table in my office, I read him the performance improvement plan I'd written—a document that outlined my non-negotiable terms that he had to meet by a certain date if he wanted to keep his job. I needed a stronger leader in that functional leadership role and still hoped he'd step up. It would require massive improvement.

"Chad, I've put together a performance improvement plan. I need the quality systems strengthened." I slid a six-page document across the table that explained the who, what, and when of the improvements needed in the department. "Go ahead and read this document."

The document didn't discuss how we would create improvement. It was Chad's job to create the plan.

"I'm going to be out of a job in ninety days, right?" said Chad.

"Not necessarily," I answered. "You'll stay in this position if you demonstrate adequate progress. That's up to you."

"I don't know how to improve the department. If I did, I would have done so already," he said.

Chad didn't have the growth mindset required for that critical role. He'd been promoted into a position he wasn't suited for, and the results during his three years in that role were the proof. I coached him to expand his knowledge and skillset to strengthen the organization, but he didn't have the drive to do it. After the first thirty days, he became distant.

On the ninetieth day, I called him into my office and said that since he hadn't executed the performance improvement plan, he was being terminated. Chad's shoulders slumped. I told him that I'd tried to find him another position in the organization for which he was qualified, but there weren't any openings. His shoulders slumped further.

Like a death march, we walked to his office together to collect his personal items, and he shook hands with those he knew well on the manufacturing floor. When he arrived at the quality office, he said goodbye to his direct reports, Gary and Jon. These guys had grown close in their personal relationships, and it was sad to watch them say goodbye. I walked Chad to the door with his small box of personal items and told him I'd keep an eye and ear out for any positions that might be a good fit.

Letting Chad go was a necessary move for the organization, but it wasn't easy from a personal perspective.

I set a new level of quality expectations in the plant. The first step was to remove an ineffective leader. I hired a new person who assumed full authority and responsibility for the quality department. Chad's replacement had a background in process improvement, quality control, ISO program management, and an insatiable desire to reduce variability. It was a good move, but it took years to realize the full benefits from this change in a function where predictability and error-rate reduction is the desired outcome.

The new leader started out strong. She took immediate ownership of the audits, workflows, and results. I left the organization about a year later, but when I checked back, the quality metrics were still headed in the right direction, and the vision continued as planned.

Leaders who suffer from imposter syndrome are out of alignment or unaware of their strengths. Your strengths are your keys to success. But you might find yourself in a role that isn't aligned with your strengths and, therefore, exposes debilitating weaknesses. Since you feel inadequate, you try to be all things to all people and be good at everything, and then you feel like what you're good at isn't enough to make and keep you successful

Leaders who suffer from imposter syndrome are out of alignment or unaware of their strengths. To close the gap, take a personal inventory of skills and place them into the three buckets: strengths, non-strengths, and debilitating weaknesses.

To close the gap, take a personal inventory of skills and place them into the three buckets: strengths, non-strengths, and debilitating weaknesses. Using this inventory, you can have an honest conversation with yourself. Next, have an honest conversation with those you support—and who are supporting you—to help them better understand you. Finally, live in your strengths as close to 100 percent of the time as possible. Doing these steps will create magical results.

Develop Candid Relationships

It was an intense day. I was the evening shift manager of Tektronix electronic service depot operations, and I walked in the door at 2:00 p.m. I was scheduled to meet my new boss, the senior manager hired to coordinate the seven production managers. We met in a conference room with glass doors. Whiteboards with technical electronic diagrams and information from brainstorming sessions hung on every wall.

"Hi, I'm Brad," he said as he extended his hand and shook mine. He looked charismatic, physically healthy, and friendly.

I choked out, "Great to meet you, Brad. I'm Mike Kitko." I was thirty-five and a professional, and I still shrank in the presence of authority.

"The team tells me that you're the energy and the positivity around here. Good. I appreciate that and look forward to getting to know you," Brad said.

He continued, "I'll tell you a bit about myself. I'm not an electronics guy. I work best when I create systems, analyze data, and improve the overall structure of production flows. I'm good with people but better behind a computer, and I rely on my team to overcome my shortcomings. I'd rather hide out with technology than engage people."

I was shocked. Within minutes, Brad had told me his strengths and acknowledged his weaknesses. He was vulnerable in a way I'd never witnessed in a leader before. I did the same in return, confident and comfortable that Brad wouldn't use my weaknesses against me.

My time working with Brad was the only period in my corporate career when I felt adequate. During my career, I shrank from others and never acknowledged or expressed my limitations. I was never honest with myself or others. With Brad, I shared a solid, candid, professional relationship. In hindsight, our vulnerability and honesty made all the difference.

Brad taught me valuable lessons about authenticity and vulnerability. He demonstrated that when you acknowledge imperfections, it allows others to do the same. I never felt that I needed to put on a show with him. I was real. He expected me to be me. He used a personal approach, we connected, and the results over the next few years demonstrated the power of authenticity.

Brad knew I craved growth. He knew I was ambitious and, ultimately, sought his position. Even so, he was my greatest cheerleader. We shared a solid professional relationship based on integrity, honesty, and trust. I told him all of my fears, doubts, and concerns about my performance. He coached me, taught me, and guided me along my journey. When I asked to have my MBA sponsored by the company, he was my champion.

Soon after Brad was hired, we were in the middle of a recession, and our company—where I'd worked for over ten years—was acquired by a holding company. We had seven managers, five too many for an organization of sixty-five production employees. I held my breath during the aggressive organizational downsizing that spanned twelve months.

It was common to walk into work and find out that another member of the production management team had been let go.

One by one, we lost these managers until we were down to three, and then one of my peers was reassigned to another part of the organization. We'd started with seven and ended with two, and I was still in the mix.

"Mike, I kept you because of your skills, talents, and ambition. I trust and appreciate you, and you're the future leader of this organization," Brad reassured me.

I made the cut, round after round.

A few weeks after Brad assured me that I was his successor, I arrived for work for my normal shift.

"Mike, can I speak with you?" Karen, the regional service manager and Brad's boss, asked me right after I sat down at my desk to begin my workday.

It was a long, fifty-foot walk, and I followed Karen to the closest conference room. Thoughts of my family flashed through my mind. My girls were five and three years old, and I felt panicked about our livelihood. Beads of sweat formed on my bald head, and I felt a cold sensation on my spine like the worst scenario possible was about to unfold.

Karen pulled the door shut in the same conference room where Brad and I had first met.

"Mike," she said, "I let Brad go today due to budget cuts. The cuts are over now, and I'll meet with the rest of our team later this week. I want you to lead your team. There won't be any more changes until we all meet and discuss."

This was devastating news. I'd never connected with a boss before I met Brad—and I'd never been as successful. A deep sense of sadness washed over me.

A few months later, Karen was reassigned. The manager who replaced her was harder edged, and he had a no-nonsense approach that I'd only experienced in the Marine Corps. I shrank because I'd had three leaders in a short time. The lessons Brad taught me about vulnerability and honesty faded, but years later, I recalled them, and they anchored some valuable lessons.

For the next eight years, I played pretend and kept my mask over my inner weaknesses. When I began my journey to find inner strength in 2016, I reflected back to Brad. I remembered how transparency had created transparency and how his brutal honesty helped me overcome my own limitations. I respected Brad because he was transparent and vulnerable at all times. This lesson served me well.

———

On a random day in June of 2016, I finished my seventieth exercise session in a row. I walked out of my basement and onto my back patio. I was out of breath. I gasped for breath as if I'd just finished a marathon. Sweat dripped from my head and onto my shirt. I sat down at my patio table; my anxiety was off the charts. I hit record on my phone's video camera.

"Hey guys, this is Mike. I've always been scared to death to do this. I hated the thought of getting myself out there in front of people. I hid behind messages on Facebook, and I hid behind a false personality, and I hid behind strength I didn't have. I hid behind everything. I was afraid of everything."

That was my first real emergence. I acknowledged that I'd been living a lie, and I was done with that lie. I posted the video to Facebook and YouTube for the world to see. From that point on, my life was different. Since then, I've been vulnerable and have shared what happens in my life.

At a speaking engagement in Alton, Illinois in 2018 in front of two hundred fifty entrepreneurs, I took the microphone to introduce myself.

"My name is Mike Kitko, and I'm an executive self-mastery coach. For forty-three years, I led multi-million-dollar organizations and had no self-worth or self-esteem and felt completely inadequate in just about everything I did."

I pointed to my wife Angie in the aisle seat of the fifth row and continued. "Because I hated myself, I physically, mentally, emotionally, and sexually abused my wife Angie, and I mentally, emotionally, and sometimes physically abused my children. Hurt people hurt people. Finally, I healed my childhood trauma and emotional pain that caused that pain. Now, executive business leaders hire me to help them feel as powerful and successful inside as they appear to those they lead." I spoke with confidence and courage. I hid nothing.

Afterward, people lined up to tell me that they appreciated my vulnerability and transparency. Being honest about my story made hundreds of other people feel normal in their own fears and pain. They thanked me for exposing my emotions, heart, and soul for all to experience.

Imposters keep their deepest fears, doubts, and weaknesses hidden because they're insecure in their abilities and feel a sense of inadequacy most of the time.

Imposters keep their deepest fears, doubts, and weaknesses hidden because they're insecure in their abilities and feel a sense of inadequacy most of the time. You think everything will fall apart if you expose your fears. Sometimes you demonstrate external power and strength to compensate for your lack of internal power and strength. You're afraid to expose yourself to those you lead because you're protecting your darkness and shadow. And yet, your shadow is healed by shining light on the darkness.

Once you become vulnerable, you never need to hide again, and you invite people to meet and support you where you are. You allow others to feel normal. Vulnerable leaders allow those they lead to feel normal within their own imperfections. Being vulnerable creates personal power and strengthens everyone in their organization.

Vulnerability is like a superpower. It requires no cape, but it takes courage to step out and lead.

Chapter 3 Work

Are You Showing Up For Yourself?

1. Would you rather succeed with others or fail by yourself? Why? What's getting in the way of seeking support?

2. How are your talents aligned with your current role or position? Is your day effortless, or do you feel struggle and resistance in some tasks?

3. Do you hold the belief that to be valuable in your role and in life that some tasks must be difficult? Do you believe that struggle creates character?

4. What do you do better than anyone else?

5. Name the people in your life with whom you can be 100 percent honest at all times.

Try This!

1. Find someone you trust with whom you can be completely honest and transparent. Being 100 percent honest, let them know your deepest fears and concerns. Ask them to tell you what traits they see in you that could help offset those fears.

2. Make a list of your strengths, non-strengths, and potential debilitating weaknesses. List the activities that are critical to success in your current role or position. Compare the lists to check if your strengths are aligned with your position. Share the results with your trusted advisor. Take steps to neutralize all non-strengths and debilitating weaknesses. Remain in your strengths as close to 100 percent of the time as possible. Increase over time.

3. In normal conversation, slowly reveal the things you've kept hidden away to those people who are critical to your success and the people you spend the most time with. Discover the power and acceptance of vulnerability. If you spend a lot of time with someone and can't safely open up, perhaps it isn't healthy to have them that close to you.

Be Authentic.

I spent a long time doing what I hated.

I spent a long time being who I'm not.

It ultimately took losing my fake identities, one at a
time, with failure after failure, to realize that those
identities were not the path to happiness.

Massive income. Gone.

Big job titles. Gone

Health. Gone.

Cool guy out-drinking everyone else. Gone.

Family unity and harmony. Gone.

Happiness....

... not a shred remaining.

I somehow learned at an early age that I needed to be
fake—to show people what I thought they wanted to
see from me—to be special and successful.

I was wrong, and I failed.

But I still knew what I enjoyed in life: inspiring people.
Motivating people.

Pushing people to be their best... even though I wasn't
my best or even close to that.

I love being in front of a room and pushing people to
push themselves.

See, I've always held this dream. I've dreamed of moving
millions of people to escape their fake identities and
current realities and live the life of their dreams.

I dream that people will wake up and realize that they're
more than what most of us believe is the "way it's
supposed to be."

I dream that people will leverage their strengths, their
gifts, and their inner beauty, and face the world from
a place of happiness, not as a robot-like nine-to-fiver
that we believe we must be.

I aspire to help people free themselves from the shackles
they placed on themselves that caused them to feel
that they had no power, no options, no ability to
realize their own dreams.

I aspire to cause millions to realize that they're more
than the false beliefs about life that their surroundings
taught them before the age of ten when they could not
filter others' beliefs from their own.

For years, I lived the same life as everyone else, the
robot-like chase for material happiness that causes
massive suffering. Happiness can never be found in
materials but only by living a life true to your being,
your true nature, your purpose...

Materials are not the problem, but expecting to find
ultimate happiness in materials will cause a life-long
chase that will never end in happiness.

An escape from misery can be found in materials—but
not happiness.

True happiness can be found in living your true nature.

To help others move toward their goals, I needed to move
toward mine.

God, the universe, source energy—whatever you want
to believe or name our creator—ultimately ended my
masquerade.

To create, you must destroy.

Now I travel my true path. My beautiful, lush, green path,
full of happiness, hope, opportunity, and potential.

I follow my happiness. Not someone else's.

I follow my happiness to encourage and show others how
to follow theirs. I inspire others—sometimes with my
own tough love—to break out of their self-imposed
limitations.

I take steps toward my goal and away from the false
reality I allowed to consume me.

I meet and speak with many people daily. Most people are
living my old life with full belief in their false reality.

That their false reality—their own captivity—is the way
to happiness.

I seek to help, but some have convinced themselves that
they are no more than their suffering, their captivity,
their limitations.

They hold on to their suffering as their identity,
convinced they are no more.

I hurt for them, but that's their journey toward failure.
We need to experience our failures to figure out what
we don't desire from life.

We need the pain to enjoy the happiness.

But when they're ready to release their suffering, their
captivity, their self-imposed bondage...

...I'm ready with open arms.

I'll show them that they're more than their suffering and
limitations.

They're limitless as long as they don't limit themselves.

Today, I follow my dreams. Where once I thought my
dreams were impossible, now I move closer and closer
toward them every day.

I feel it.

And this journey has cost me much.

It cost me my past, fake identity.

I needed to be willing to give up my past self to allow the
possibility of a greater future self.

Today, I move toward my dreams. I will allow no one to
hold me back.

How will you face the day?

Are you going to a job you hate to exchange time for dollars,
or are you using your talents, strengths, gifts... and
dreams of moving the world and your dreams forward?

Are you exchanging your happiness for dollars, or are
you allowing your happiness to generate income?

If you're exchanging your time for money, at the expense
of your happiness...

...you've put yourself in handcuffs.

And you hold the key.
My dream is to help you use the key.
The choice is yours. I've made my choice, and I'm being
    rewarded daily as I see my dreams move closer.
Are yours moving closer, or do you see them move
    further away as your handcuffs get tighter and
    tighter as your life slips by day by day?
The choice is yours. Don't blame anyone else. Not God,
    not life, not family, not friends...Only you.
The choice is yours.
Are you ready?

CHAPTER 4
APPRECIATE WHAT YOU'VE ACCOMPLISHED.

We're taught to set big goals based on wealth and the ideals of success, materials, and accomplishments. When we achieve our goals and still feel unfulfilled, it's because we were never excited about our goals or the path that took us there.

There's a reason why we may not feel fulfilled and complete when we actually achieve something. It's because we sacrifice our immediate happiness to achieve goals and don't execute in ways that are in alignment with our strengths and talents. We trade real joy *now* for perceived joy *later*. Later joy never comes if we can't enjoy today.

Why don't we take aligned action? Because we aren't clear about our internal or external purpose.

Why aren't we clear? Because we lack confidence in ourselves.

Why don't we have confidence in ourselves? Because we aren't radically aware of our strengths, gifts, talents, and true desires.

It's the lack of self-awareness that keeps you from deeply appreciating yourself. You're probably setting arbitrary goals that don't motivate you. You want recognition according to the material definition of success, not your own internal definition, but it's your own internal definition of success that can lead you to happiness. The material definition of success leads to sacrifice, pain, emptiness, and time spent on activities that don't feed your soul. You may think that if you align with material goals, you'll find happiness. But this is a trap. Insanity.

I always found a way to diminish my accomplishments. I said things like:

"I happened to be in the right spot at the right time."

"Anybody could have done that."

"I'm not celebrating. It's not a big deal."

The goals hadn't been mine. The path wasn't mine. So, the accomplishments weren't mine, either. Early in my corporate career, I abused myself mentally and emotionally by dismissing any recognition I got for my development or results. I gave everyone else credit for my achievements. I explained away my own success. I dismissed my own results and promotions as good timing or chance.

I never stopped to understand myself, why I existed, what made me tick, my zone of genius, my thoughts, feelings, emotions, my past, my aligned vision, and why I felt inadequate and like an imposter every step of my life. When we don't know ourselves at a deep level, we can't live an authentic life.

Leaders who feel like an imposter often live someone else's vision, dreams, and ambitions.

Leaders who feel like an imposter often live someone else's vision, dreams, and ambitions. You accept promotions to grasp for the feeling of happiness and success. You accept a role because it's what someone else envisioned for you or it will impress your parents or other significant figures in your life through your power and prestige. And the entire time, you feel like an imposter.

The solution is to get clear and honest with yourself about your own dreams and to step into them. When you appreciate what you have instead of obsessing over what you don't have, you'll experience joy, peace, and love. Happiness is always now, never later. Seek radical self-awareness, align yourself to your own inner compass, and execute to your own aligned goals.

If you can't be happy now, you won't be happy later. There is only now. Later is just now… but later. Create a life where your aligned actions created aligned outcomes. That's where you'll find true fulfillment.

When you appreciate what you have instead of obsessing over what you don't have, you'll experience joy, peace, and love. Happiness is always now, never later.

Gain Radical Self-Awareness

When I start working with a new client, they learn that their physical well-being, mental clarity, and emotional courage generate outcomes and determine how they show up in the world. They realize that their current lifestyle and choices have created their current realities, and meaningful, healthy choices bring meaningful, healthier outcomes. I ask them about their past and help them see how their shadow—those things about themselves they'd rather hide or forget—shows up in their current thoughts, feelings, and emotions.

This discovery often begins the long, steady process of radical self-awareness. We dive into deeper levels of knowingness, never settling for the current state, but recognizing that the current state allows us to determine the false beliefs, thoughts, feelings, and emotions that don't bring us happiness and internal peace. My clients understand that their current state has been created out of fear or feelings of limitation, and we work to resolve those that need the most attention.

I met Tony G., a successful business executive, in 2017.

"They keep promoting me, and I don't know why," Tony said with a smile on his face and doubt in his voice. "I'm not sure what they see in me, but everyone backs me and supports me."

"What do they praise you for?" I asked.

"Everything. My presence, my leadership, my public speaking, my results. Everything. I don't see the same things they see," Tony answered.

I dug deeper, "Do you believe you're as good as they tell you?"

"I guess so. Not really. I feel like I'm doing my job." Tony reflected.

Patrons came in and out of the local cafe. It was near the end of the work day, and the number of people in the cafe had doubled since we started our conversation. It was busy.

"What happened in your life that caused you to feel that you were never good enough?" I asked.

"Parents," Tony answered. My parents rewarded my brother's athletic abilities, and I wasn't athletic. I was the intellectual kid, and the fact that I wasn't athletic was a disappointment to them. I was never good enough."

"You've rejected your own gifts because they were never good enough for your parents. Do you see how you've carried out their beliefs?" I said as we both recognized the work that needed to be done.

Tony was confused because he felt like an imposter even though he'd been consistently promoted and received great reviews. People saw in him what he couldn't feel, and even though he was given accolades for his public speaking abilities, he felt anxiety weeks before any speaking event. Tony's leadership, presence, and drive led to his success. But he didn't know how or why. He was uncomfortable when his bosses, peers, and team poured praise on him. He deflected and minimized the praise, insisting that performance was part of his job and that his talents were average.

Tony recognized that he expected perfection from himself, and that expectation created pain because it was impossible to achieve. He also recognized that, at times, he expected perfection from those around him, which caused them frustration and stress. His early experiences taught him that nothing was good enough, and this feeling was present in all facets of his life, including his relationships, finances, job performance, and lack of satisfaction. He couldn't appreciate himself.

When we began our work, Tony said he wanted to understand what people saw in him and to feel the power of his talents. He wanted to reduce his anxiety before presentations and speaking engagements, and he wanted to lower the expectations he had of himself and others so he could reduce his level of frustration.

Since we knew the root of his disconnect, we dove deeper into the aspects of himself that he rejected. He knew he didn't have a pleasant childhood, but he didn't realize how much his past was influencing his current mental and emotional state. I helped him connect the dots so he could see that his quest for perfection was an attempt to please his parents and that the parental disappointment he tried to overcome in his childhood was still alive and well, and it was driving his behavior.

Through self-reflection, Tony acknowledged his talents and what others saw in him. He's driven and fast-paced. He's a strong and gifted leader. He built self-awareness by journaling and through an honest connection with his shadow. He practiced mirror work, which is a face-to-face conversation with yourself about your deepest fears and highest truths. As you face your-self during mirror work, it drives new awareness and lessons straight into the nervous system.

Together, we created lists of talents and skills to understand his zone of genius. We differentiated his talents and successes from other successful leaders' talents and successes. When you see that your uniqueness creates and drives success, it becomes harder to minimize yourself. We built a safe environment for Tony to speak with increased ease and honesty about his fears and perceived limitations, as well as boast about his accomplishments. With work, Tony felt each of his accomplishments in his body and tied these accomplishments to talents and gifts he possessed.

We discussed the strengths that people recognized and the emotional resistance he experienced when he acknowledged these strengths. I taught Tony some meditative techniques, breathing exercises, and visualization exercises to replace the anxiety and fear he stored in his body.

Tony sought to become more comfortable speaking in front of an audience. He was a gifted speaker, but his anxiety was excessive even months before a presentation.

"What's the topic of the presentation, Tony?" I asked to gain clarity.

Tony responded, "I'll be debriefing all of the changes that I've made to my staff, processes, and my vision. I'll speak to the entire organization."

"Sit with yourself for ten to twenty minutes a day and visualize speaking to the audience. Don't worry about the content. Visualize the audience clapping, nodding in approval, and congratulating you on a great presentation," I advised.

"And that will help?" he expressed with skepticism.

"It will. Anxiety is formed by past events and memories. When you visualize outcomes, you rewire your brain to recognize a new, preferred outcome. When you repeat the visualization, your body will realign with the new visualization," I said.

Tony agreed after hesitating and resisting. "Okay. I'll do it, but it's going to take some getting used to."

We debriefed each week on his wins and challenges and focused on celebrating the wins. I poured praise, affirmation, and recognition on Tony. I continued to say the four magic words human beings have a deep desire to hear: I believe in you.

Your presence, choices, beliefs, thoughts, and actions attract your outcomes, both positive and negative. When you don't recognize this, you must unpack and unravel each event to determine how they created and caused the outcome. You'll find that connection if you inquire with intention. When you discover that you created a negative outcome, it brings liberation because you can accept responsibility for the positive outcomes of the past and all future outcomes.

Together, Tony and I discovered why the feelings of inadequacy and rejection he adopted as a child caused him to doubt himself as an adult. When you bring the reasons for your suffering and inner conflict to your awareness, the struggles can begin to heal.

Tony was armed with new tools and awareness to accept himself as he was designed, which could heal his anxieties. His current emotions were false signals of failure and rejection. He could lead with a present awareness of the strengths and gifts he was given at birth.

"Well, my friend, this isn't the last time we'll connect," I said to open our final video conference call. "I appreciate you too much to let you go that easily."

"You have helped me so much, Mike." Tony acknowledged.

"How is life different?" I asked.

"I show up knowing who I am and what I'm capable of achieving. I know my gifts and talents. I care more about those who accept me than those who don't. People who don't accept me aren't significant enough in my life to worry about," he said, glowing as he spoke.

"And how do you show up now?" I asked.

"I am who I am, and I'm enough," Tony closed.

That last call was brief with high levels of mutual admiration. We reflected on his thoughts, doubts, and feelings before we began our work compared to his new state. Tony recognized that he's a gifted leader, that he has a powerful leadership presence, and that he's a powerful speaker. He feels that when he speaks, people listen and believe in and follow him because he expects excellence, but now with a loving touch.

He's minimized his expectations of perfection because he understands that these expectations were created in childhood. He's gained more compassion for others and tries to understand their challenges. Challenges invite opportunities for him to coach his staff toward growth.

While we worked together, Tony received another promotion, and he reorganized the team to complement his strengths, talents, vision, and expectation of excellence. He executed this reorganization with grace, ease, and confidence, aware that his leadership is powerful, empowers people, and drives results. Tony says he still experiences minor anxiety before speaking, which is healthy, but it no longer paralyzes him weeks before.

Even powerful leaders hold on to painful trauma and experiences from the past. You often run from these past experiences, and this shows up in your behavior. Leaders who experience imposter syndrome relive past traumas. We're all perfectly imperfect. Imposters feel that everyone else is whole while you feel broken. None of us are broken. Getting radically self-aware will help you find the light in your shadow and will help you heal the painful past that causes your self-doubts and judgment.

Leaders who experience imposter syndrome relive past traumas. We're all perfectly imperfect. Imposters feel that everyone else is whole while you feel broken. None of us are broken.

Find Your Inner Compass

"My name is Mike Kitko, and I own Hope Works Partnership. My agency works with employers and assists their laid-off or terminated employees find another job after their exit," I said as I introduced myself and my business to a florist.

I formed Hope Works Partnership soon after my second termination. At that time, I felt lost and looked for a job and some quick income, so I figured I'd help others with a similar plight. I walked a busy commercial district and introduced myself to business owners to see if I could get some quick feedback and business.

I handed my brand-new business card to the owner of the flower shop. She looked at my shiny card, paused, then looked at the logo on my new shirt that I was wearing for the first time.

"How long have you been in business?" she asked.

With anxiety and embarrassment, I replied, "Formed about a month ago."

"Why help people land on their feet?" she questioned with some cynicism.

"Because I was terminated and felt lost and alone, and there was no one to help me. I want to help others avoid that loneliness and depression," I said, embarrassed that my words and internal feelings didn't match.

At that point, I couldn't have cared less about helping people get another job or land on their feet. I opened Hope Works

Partnership as a scarcity and desperation move while I searched for a job. I felt pressure to make some quick income, so I pulled the first idea out of my ass and moved into action. That was the first and last time I ever tried to promote Hope Works Partnership. The brand and idea died.

Meanwhile, I applied for every job I was qualified for and went on a few interviews. I followed any path I could find to begin the flow of money. I sorely lacked the clarity to know what I wanted and the confidence to believe I could achieve it.

––––––

Confidence, courage, and clarity of purpose are the bridges between self-awareness and goal attainment. Confidence and courage aren't what you possess after you achieve. They're what enable you to achieve. Imposters are often fueled by the "fake it until you make it" mentality, but there's a difference between confidence and competence. You can become competent while being self-confident, but you can't achieve sustained self-confidence with competence alone.

> Imposters are often fueled by the "fake it until you make it" mentality, but there's a difference between confidence and competence. You can become competent while being self-confident, but you can't achieve sustained self-confidence with competence alone.

This lesson came clear many years after I "made it," but never shed the feeling of being an imposter. The trauma and neglect of my childhood drove my lack of confidence and courage, which led me to have no clarity about my purpose. After I built my self-awareness, I needed to build a sense of confidence in myself, and from this confidence, new purpose emerged. I never thought—not in a million years—that I could coach, speak, write a book, or build an organization capable of serving so many.

Sustained confidence requires you to engage in the process of physical, mental, and emotional development that's in alignment with your highest purpose. It's a process that brings instant results. Confidence and courage come from the awareness that you're as valuable and worthy as anyone else. No one is expendable. You establish your value and worth when you act in your best interest, from your point of authenticity, with strong boundaries established and protected for your own well-being. You're here to serve others and, except for those who agree to risk their lives as their profession, we aren't here to sacrifice our own well-being for the well-being of others.

The worth and value you feel establishes your confidence, courage, and clarity, which enables you to find your purpose. Purpose drives significance.

———

"Would you coach executive leaders?" my good friend, Art Snarzyk, asked casually.

"I can't do that!" I answered.

"Why not?" Art asked as he unpacked more of my doubts and fears.

Art owns Inner View Advisors, and he's also known as the Turnover Terminator because he's a genius at helping companies hire the right people for their culture and aligned skill set. Art recognizes talent.

I responded with great emotion. "Because I failed. I can't coach others when I couldn't even help myself."

"That's why you should coach them," Art said. "There's no one who can help them better than you. Have you ever recognized any success in your career?"

"A lot of success," I said.

"Have you ever failed?" Art asked with a direct stare and a sharp tone.

"You know I have," I responded with a why-waste-my-time tone in my voice.

"If you've experienced success, and you've experienced failure as an executive, and you love to coach, don't you think you'd be the best person to coach other executives?" Art asked.

I saw the logic in his statement but could not feel alignment with that logic. I knew I wanted to coach power players, but it seemed like a stretch. I contemplated my target audience, and it didn't feel natural to coach at the highest level.

"As an executive, what kept you up at night?" Art continued.

That was easy. "Feeling like I didn't have a firm grasp on things, like I was out of control. I struggled to feel the power and authority I held in every position."

"There it is, Mike. Haven't you learned to feel your power?" Art asked.

"I have," I replied.

"You can help executives overcome that same feeling. They need you," Art said, certain he'd helped me determine my future.

————

Before I began my journey, it seemed like a waste of time to consider my hopes and dreams. I felt average in every way. I'd held a good title, earned a solid income, and possessed lots of material wealth, but in my mind, anyone could have achieved that. I sacrificed every day. Because my level of internal significance was rock-bottom, my happiness mattered less than everyone else's Significant people were talented; I was not.

I was depressed, and my life reflected it. I woke up when I didn't want to, I went somewhere I didn't want to go, I did activities I didn't want to do, and I worked for someone I didn't want to work for. I felt that's all I deserved. That's just the way life was. At least I wasn't poor and unhappy.

What you lack inside, you expect others to provide for you. What you feel unable to provide for yourself, you need from others. I couldn't find happiness or joy for myself, so I looked to everyone else to provide it. I needed others because I felt I couldn't stand alone. This showed up at work, at home, in my friendships, and in my internal mental and emotional state. For forty-three years, I ran like this. I behaved at forty-three how a five-year-old child behaves when mom and dad are the source of everything.

I tried to keep everyone satisfied and give them what they wanted, so I could squeeze all that I needed from them. My giving was selfish. I couldn't afford to lose the painful identity I'd created because I didn't know who I'd be without it. I didn't know there was any more to life than mental and emotional dependency.

When I look back to my corporate career, I see that I was always a coach first. "Who do you want to be when you grow up?" I asked Mitch, one of my employees at Kemlab Production Components, a small defense manufacturing plant in St. Louis that I managed in 2015. Mitch was a talented machining supervisor. I was curious about him, his desires, and how I could help him advance toward his goal.

"I don't know," Mitch replied.

"Well, what do you love to do most?" I asked.

"I teach people how to be physically fit," he said. "I teach them to run and work out to increase their fitness."

"You do this now?" I dug deeper.

"I do!" he said with genuine excitement. "I meet people on Saturday mornings and take them on runs with me."

"Why don't you charge them for it and make a business out of it?" I said.

"Do you think I can do that?" he asked in a shocked tone.

"Is there anyone else who charges for the same thing?" I asked.

Mitch thought for a second and replied, "Many. There are a lot of professionals who train other people."

"Then, why not you? I concluded.

Mitch looked puzzled. We had many more conversations about the potential of his new business venture in the months ahead until I was fired from Kemlab. It was the termination that reset my life.

In my various roles, I'd helped my employees align their lives to create a more authentic, prosperous life. Most people who worked for me were trading time for money, and I knew they would do something else if they could. So regardless of my role and relationship, I took time and convinced them to follow their dreams. There were even a few who took the leap and succeeded!

After I was terminated from Kemlab in March of 2016, I faced the same doubts and fears I'd challenged others to overcome. In my conversation with Art, he helped me gain clarity about who I coached and what challenges I helped them overcome. But those doubts and fears were still ever-present.

The way I gain clarity and confidence is to sit in reflection and in "feeling into" what I want. When I sit still in absolute quiet and visualize the outcome I desire, I can identify the doubts, fears, and concerns I carry. I keep an inventory of these doubts, fears, and concerns, and I try to find out where I've established false beliefs in my life. I ask myself, *Does this apply to every single person, or is there at least one person to whom this doesn't apply?* If there's even one on the planet to whom this belief doesn't apply, then it's a belief that can be modified. If it's true for all people—like being a human who isn't designed to fly unassisted—then it's a truth, not a belief. You must separate belief from truth to see clearly.

For example, you need a lot of start-up money, and you must assume a lot of risk to start a business. This is false. Thousands of businesses were started with little to no upfront money and began with no real risk. Read the story of 1-800-Got-Junk. Brian Scudamore was a college student who wanted to earn some side money, so he bought a $700 truck and knocked on people's doors when he saw a yard full of garbage.

Brian attended college until the phone calls for junk removal disrupted his classes. He realized that his business had taken off, and it blossomed into a full-time opportunity helping people solve a problem that no one else had solved.

After I read Scudamore's story, I realized that not all new business ventures require tons of seed capital and excessive risk. It takes a problem and a problem solver. The belief that a new business must be risky is a false belief that millions of people carry around. Brian Scudamore was crazy enough and took a few small steps, and his confidence, courage, and clarity were built on the journey.

It was easy for me to launch a successful coaching business. Once I overcame my false belief that I couldn't build the business of my dreams, and I took steps toward the vision, I found confidence and clarity. My three Cs—confidence, courage, and clarity—build like a snowball grows when it's rolled across a blanket of fresh powder.

Even though I battle self-doubt and self-trust challenges daily and face them to create the most powerful version of me possible, my life's purpose burns strong, and my excitement increases each morning. When I step out of bed, I find my internal compass and face the world in full authenticity so I can teach others to do the same. I build from a place of confidence, courage, and clarity.

I get excited about things that fall under the umbrella of my purpose: to teach people how to release struggle by realigning their lives with their own inner compasses. I've been presented with investments, business ideas, and partnerships that fall outside of this purpose, and I dismiss them, not because they're bad ideas, but because my passion for them will fizzle and fade. I have clarity about my life purpose, and I stick to it.

If you listen to your soul's voice with the intention to understand, you might feel a call that is much different from the life you're living right now. If you stay in your current role because you're afraid, then chances are you feel a misalignment between your internal and external worlds. One thing that drives the imposter syndrome is a lack of alignment. You must be aligned with your own dream based on love for yourself rather than fear. To relieve this pressure and to heal the imposter syndrome, find and execute on your internal compass.

Execute to Aligned Goals

In January of 2017, I attended a presentation about creating the life of your dreams. The facilitator's name was Shaun. He asked the audience, "Who has a big goal for this year?" Many hands shot up, and Shaun singled out a guy who sat in the second row, right in front of him.

"What's your goal?" Shaun asked.

"Hit $945k in profit from real estate this year," the young, tall fella answered in a confident and powerful voice.

"That's a big goal! How did you come up with that number?"

"That's the number I'm confident I can hit if I remain focused," he answered.

Shaun thought a second and said, "So based on your previous sales and experience, you believe $945k is realistic."

"Exactly," the guy said.

"I know you did the math because if you were shooting from the hip, you would have rounded up to $1 million," Shaun said, impressed.

"I thought about it," the young man said, with a confident smile and powerful posture.

Shaun began, "How many hours are you going to work per week to make that number?"

"Between sixty to seventy hours per week on average," replied the burgeoning real estate tycoon.

Shaun dug deeper "So you're going to average sixty to seventy hours of work-related activity per week. I assume you'll give up some of your personal life. You have your sights set on $945k in profit, and when you make it, you'll be happy with your life and outcome?"

"I will," said the young man.

"Will you be happy if you hit $845k?" Shaun countered.

"No," replied the driven fella.

"Why not?" Shaun asked.

Without flinching, the young man replied, "Because that won't hit my goal."

"Your goal means that much to you?" Shaun asked.

"It does. I dream about it," he said.

"Okay, so let's not talk about your goal. Let's talk about your lifestyle. If you hit $845k, will you have a decent lifestyle?" Shaun asked.

"A good lifestyle," he answered.

"How about $500k? Would you have a decent lifestyle with $500k?" Shaun asked.

"Still good," he replied. He understood where Shaun was headed with his questions.

"How about $300k?" Shaun said with an eyebrow raised and a funny look on his face which drew a laugh.

"Good," the young man said as he blushed.

"How about $200k? Could you live a decent lifestyle with a profit of $200k this year?" Shaun asked, confident he knew the answer.

Shattered, the young man responded, "Yes. I'd still live a good lifestyle."

Shaun folded his arms and paused. With his eyebrow still raised, he said, "Let me ask. How much is the most you've ever made in your life in a year?"

The young man, who was about twenty-six years old, paused for a second, glanced at his friend next to him, and replied, "I made $125k last year."

"And the year before that?" Shaun asked.

"$80k," the man replied, embarrassed.

"And you wouldn't be happy with $845k because you wouldn't have hit your goal? Are you serious? You'll give up an entire year of your life for an arbitrary number? You'll sacrifice your life now—the best years of your life—for a life later?" Shaun asked with excitement.

"I guess that was my plan," he replied, a bit deflated from the original power and confidence he'd demonstrated at first.

Shaun took a breath. "And that's why we're here. This isn't about who can set the biggest goals and hit them. We're going to talk about goals that allow you to live your life now and goals that will allow you to continue living your life going forward."

It was a brilliant demonstration of how we form goals based on ego and pride rather than alignment and logic.

———

I met Corey in 2017. He negotiates and buys thirty properties a year to rehab and resale, and he never struggles to generate a six-figure income. I labeled Corey's ability to earn that kind of income his financial "easy" button (think Staples). Along with his charm, charisma, athletic physique, and huge smile, you'd say that Corey has it all.

"What do you want to achieve?" I asked Corey.

"I feel broken, like I'm not fixable. I've hired a few coaches, but they couldn't help me," he said, a bit depressed.

Corey liked to listen to motivational speakers to gain an edge. (My wife, Angie, calls them "Hustle Whores" and "Grind Gurus.") They emphasized sacrificing your time, happiness, and life in general for financial gain and wealth. So Corey didn't do anything fun because when he did, he felt guilt and shame because he didn't want to grind. Instead, he wanted to make enough money from investing in real estate to build a photography business, travel, and do the simple things in life. He valued peace and happiness above the grind. While we worked together, he bought a ticket to a "Grind Guru" weekend in Las Vegas.

After he returned, I asked, "How was your time away?"

He dipped a half sandwich in his cup of tomato bisque and replied, "I felt broken before, and I feel even more broken now."

"I know there was a lot of energy there.," I said. "Why do you feel more broken?"

"I don't want what they want. Thousands of people were there, and they were all about getting rich and giving up everything to make millions. The crowd went crazy every time someone mentioned sacrifice now for rewards later. I want to enjoy my life *now*. I feel broken. I feel like I should want what they want," he said.

I looked him dead in the eyes, waiting for him to continue. I knew we'd just made progress. Corey became more self-aware with every statement. Sometimes people need to hear themselves express their own feelings out loud to feel their own chaos.

Why don't I care to be rich as much as everybody else?" Corey said with zero energy.

I paused and took a breath. "Great question. I'm glad you realize that you're not like everyone else."

We dove into who Corey was, his talents and gifts, his values, his vision, his goals, and why his own goals didn't feel adequate to him.

"Let's align on this, Corey. You're not broken. You're not everyone else, and you shouldn't want what everyone wants. You need to get clear about what you want, why you want it, and become satisfied with your own goals and desires," I told him. "What do you want?"

"I want to feel like I don't need chemicals to make me feel normal. I want to feel like I can open a photography business. I want to earn enough in real estate to fund my life and travel. I don't want to need more than I have, I want to have what I need to do everything I want to do," he said, intense sadness in his voice. "I want to feel normal wanting what I want!"

Corey compared his pain, guilt, and shame to everyone else's success. He didn't realize that everyone has a shadow; he thought he was the only one who felt pain. Actually, everyone feels pain and has a shadow, but not everyone else expresses or shows that pain. Ego and fear keep people from fully expressing their deepest secrets. Some individuals, especially those who are covering up internal pain, only allow others to see the good, not the pain and suffering they endure.

We continued to investigate what Corey wanted. We began a self-mastery journey and focused on his physical, mental, and emotional development. Over a few months, Corey shed a few chemicals and his unhealthy addiction to social attention he'd relied on to sedate his emotions. He replaced bad habits with good ones, and as he felt complete again, he announced his new photography business in a social media post. The positive responses and demand overwhelmed him.

Because of his improved health, outlook on life, easy button for income, and new photography business, Corey stepped into what life could be as he defined it, not as others defined it for him. We established some basic expectations about how much time he should spend on real estate, photography, and other beneficial activities. He gave himself permission to release his own guilt and shame and shed his need to be like other people. He chose not to adopt other people's definition of success.

I recently received a message from Corey. He was on a three-week trip to Europe. He had another week to go but looked forward to coming home. He said that two weeks away from home was a long time when you spend it roaming from place to place, living a hectic lifestyle. He'd gotten used to his routine at home that served his happiness in an aligned manner, so the trip was a bit of a challenge. He was enjoying all the sights and attractions he'd dreamed of seeing, but for the first time, he'd also tasted the simplicity and joy of living simply and doing things that made him happy. He was eager to get home to that.

When you understand and appreciate yourself, find peace in what you want for yourself, and take aligned steps toward your own unique goals, you can feel internal peace and substantial clarity. When you don't know yourself and don't align with your own desires, you might try to achieve the things that others say you should desire. Executives who lack internal clarity and chase goals that are established by others feel the chaos of being an imposter. The correct goal for you is the one that's aligned with your true nature and design. Joy comes from finding your own inner compass.

Chapter 4 Work

Are You Showing Up For Yourself?

1. Do you take credit for your accomplishments or excuse them as a coincidence or good timing?

2. Have you connected childhood trauma to your current behavior, so you can recognize your patterns and programming?

3. Do you accept all of your desires and make them the centerpiece of your life, or do you live to support someone else's dream?

4. Do your goals support your desires, or were they created to attain external acceptance or future happiness?

Try This!

1. Make a list of all of your accomplishments from your entire life. Acknowledge your role in achieving each accomplishment. Stand in front of a mirror, look yourself in the eyes, acknowledge the accomplishment, and congratulate yourself.

2. What's your earliest memory of feeling fear? What caused that fear? Consider how you have attracted or are avoiding the same conditions in your life and how that event still impacts your life today.

3. Make a list of your current goals. Consider your perfect day right now. Do your current goals allow you to live your perfect life right now? If your current goals aren't aligned with your desired life, your goals might be the problem. How can you align your goals and perfect life? How can you have happiness now and in the future? Assume you can have both, and work from there.

Awareness.

I've done a lot of work to become better.
There's still so far to go.
Do I still hurt?
More than ever.
I lean into my hurt and do nothing to numb it.
I want to feel every feeling.
Do I still have bouts of internal emotional chaos?
Fuck. Yes.
I've attained, at times, the most emotional stability I've
    ever felt, so the chaos feels even more volatile.
Do I still fuck up?
Absolutely.
I'm human. And I fail so I can learn.
Do I get upset with myself?
No doubt.
I know better but do the best I can at the moment.
Do I still project my hurts onto others?
Hurt people hurt people.
But the severity, magnitude, and length of my battles are
    much improved.
I recognize improvement by the relative control...
... which was once complete abandon of reason,
    unleashed uncontrolled anger, and absolute rage.
I'm still learning how to create effective and healthy
    boundaries to enable my best interest.
I'm still learning how to accept pain in others around me
    without being engulfed by its grasp.
I must still manage human emotions and feelings because
    I'm human.
I'm not above or better than anyone.
I'm better than I once was.
I continue to journey.
The journey begins with better.

Every challenge shows me who I am so I can address
those areas that need to be addressed.
Down but not out.
Never.
This process is a journey. Not a destination.

CHAPTER 5

KNOW WHO YOU ARE AND WHERE YOU'RE GOING.

It's estimated that 10 percent of people have a written goal or a vision to work toward. The other 90 percent either live without intention, aren't confident enough in themselves to create a goal or vision, or can't gain enough internal clarity to generate external clarity. If you're part of that 90 percent, you might need to develop internal clarity, take a breath, or take time to reflect on your vision.

When my wife and I began our journey to heal, we attended a weekend retreat to learn more about ourselves and develop a vision for our lives. We each developed our individual vision without the other's input, and we were fortunate that our visions still included each other. Before then, our lives revolved around material possessions, as if our purpose in life was to accumulate things.

———

"Can you believe this?" I asked Angie as I sat next to her on the couch.

"Believe what?" she responded in a tone that suggested she had no idea what I was thinking.

I pointed out the window as several cars backed out of their driveways to head off to work. "That!" I said with excitement. I continued to point but said nothing else.

"What are you talking about?" she asked, concerned that I'd lost my mind.

"That we sit here and watch our neighbors leave for work every day," I said.

Every morning we sit together, drink coffee, and look out our front window and watch our neighbors go to work. Sometimes we take our life for granted. We enjoy each other and the schedules we create for ourselves. We set parameters and limits on our time. We're in full control of our days. We're responsible to no one and choose our own accountability partners.

"A few years ago, you'd pull out to go to work yourself, and we thought that's how it was always going to be," Angie said.

"And I never thought this was possible," I said as I took a drink of my coffee, stood to get another cup, and watched more cars pull away from their homes.

Since our rebuild, we've realized that there's more to life than titles, wealth, and material possessions. We value our happiness, peace, and our moment-by-moment lives. We're committed to each other, and we don't sacrifice today for tomorrow. We seek consistent peace and happiness, not the false happiness that comes through things. Don't get me wrong, we appreciate nice things, but we know they can't give us any lasting feeling that we don't already possess. We believe that we continue to own nicer and nicer things because we value our happiness more than those things. The more we're grateful for what we have, the more financial freedom we experience.

———

Innate talents and gifts, inner compass, goal alignment, and seizing the day instead of sacrificing it for tomorrow—when you bring all these elements together into a single approach to life, you find magic. You're never too far from alignment to recover; you're never too invested. Freedom begins when you only need to breathe to create income. Imagine waking up and being yourself, and people pay you for your presence and talents—without you having to sacrifice. It's all available if you believe it is. It seems like a dream, but it's fully available.

Executive leaders engulfed by imposter syndrome are often living someone else's dream, never taking the time to figure out what they want or to ask if a better life is possible. The feeling of being a fraud keeps them trapped, wondering if there's more, but they're paralyzed in the secure, uncomfortable life they've created.

> **Executive leaders engulfed by imposter syndrome are often living someone else's dream, never taking the time to figure out what they want or to ask if a better life is possible.**

To determine the next step, you must understand your deepest thoughts, feelings, emotions, and desires; align your talents with your desires; and cast an aligned vision that satisfies your own soul's desires.

Understand Yourself Deeply

Everything that you've become and what you will accomplish comes back to self-awareness and self-acceptance. Addiction is prevalent in our society today because people try to sedate their thoughts, feelings, and emotions rather than understand and heal them. You'll grow when you accept and embrace who you are and discern between those things that serve and heal you and those that don't support your continued growth. From there you can choose better.

When you embrace your higher *and* lower qualities, you find self-acceptance. Through self-acceptance, you can move past the pain toward purpose. Painful things such as being an abuser, an alcoholic, or an adulterer are not things that make people proud, but when you accept them as part of the story that brought you to this point of making a choice to heal, you can see that they have served your growth. When you know better, you can do better.

"On an emotional scale from zero to ten with zero being dead, one being suicidal, and ten being enlightened like Jesus, Buddha, Krishna, and Lao Tzu, where do you fit?" I asked Andrew, eager to understand his current emotional state.

"About a six," Andrew replied.

"If you continue to beat yourself up and reject yourself as you have been, what's going to happen to that six?" I asked, wanting to find out if he knew that self-rejection creates long-term damage.

"It will move down the scale," he said.

"What happens if you choose to accept yourself?" I asked. "What would happen if you embraced your pain, your suffering, your shit, your failures, and your shortcomings? What would happen if you fully accepted yourself?"

"The six would either stay the same or move up," he said, beginning to understand the damage he'd inflicted on himself by rejecting the powerful lessons he'd learned. His perceived failures were actually his greatest gifts.

"So the sooner you drop the I-should-haves and I-wish-I-hads, the sooner the six will become a seven," I said. "And when the six becomes a seven, you'll start to attract things that a seven attracts. Or, if you prefer, you can beat yourself up and attract what a five attracts. It's your choice."

That was an "aha!" moment for Andrew, a turning point that led him to more peace in his life.

———

When you accept where you are—wherever you are—you move up the emotional scale. When you're aware of and accept your current state, you begin the process of healing and can find the positive angle in any situation. It's all about self-awareness and self-acceptance.

Spend some quality time in silence. Sit on a pillow with your legs crossed, back straight, with the top of your hands rested on your knees, palms up. This is called *easy pose*. Breath in through your nose and out through your mouth. Take deep breaths and feel the air circulating in your body. As soon as you finish your exhale, begin your inhale. Pay close attention to your breath and observe any thoughts that you have.

Be aware that underneath those thoughts are fears. Allow any fears to rest as they are. Pay special attention to any emotion you feel and allow it, without resistance. If you can, amplify the emotion and truly feel it. This could be hard for you because you've probably spent most of your life fighting your pain, suffering, fears, and emotions. Now that you're connecting with yourself, sit with it and allow. Healing will begin immediately. What you resist persists. What you feel heals.

I had pain in my childhood, like we all have, whether we're aware of it or not. I ran from that pain my entire life and kept running to the next thing, seeking relief. I expected that the next step, purchase, raise, car, or title would bring me eternal happiness. I didn't know there was any other way of being. But the pain I repressed made it nearly impossible to believe that I could create a plan, embrace a vision, or achieve a goal. I was in survival mode, so I clung to the belief that the next step or material thing would sedate the pain.

———

I walked alone through my manufacturing plant at Stanley Black & Decker. The day seemed dark. My employees were heads down in their machines, and I received a few smiles as I walked by. I felt as if they were being compliant.

The smell of machine coolant and the thickness of lubricant hung in the dense, humid air. The sound of metal cutting metal overwhelmed my unprotected eardrums, and some of the higher pitched sounds hit the deepest part of my nervous system. Machines created parts, parts built tools, and tools build everything. I was proud to be part of building our society.

My mood was dark that day. The plant seemed dark. Body language appeared dark. Wherever I looked, everything appeared negative, empty, and closed off. I looked up at the overhead lights, fifty feet in the air, and they were working fine, but the plant seemed full of darkness.

Just the day before, I'd walked the same path under the same conditions, and everything seemed bright and vivid, full of color. My employees seemed genuine. The plant seemed luminous. The laughs were louder. Smiles were warmer and more welcoming. My mood was elevated, as I perceived happiness and openness.

That day, even though the conditions were the same, everything seemed darker and closed off. The problem was me. My internal world was dark some days, light the others. The plant was the same every single day.

I craved wealth, power, titles, status, significance, loyalty, appreciation, recognition, love, and friendships, not because they complimented my life and my purpose, but because I felt like I couldn't live without them. I felt inadequate and empty as if I were nothing if I didn't have those things. I was always looking for ways to increase everything in my life as a way to find the happiness, joy, safety, security, and love I couldn't give myself.

Imposters often need things outside themselves to compensate for things they don't possess inside.

Imposters often need things outside themselves to compensate for things they don't possess inside. But once they establish themselves as their means to provide their own happiness, joy, safety, security, and love, the need for other things decreases.

When you feel joy and happiness, things outside of you are fun to attain, but they aren't necessary for survival.

————

I sat in easy pose in front of the window in my home office. The window sill is only a foot from the ground, so practically my entire body faced the glass. I sat in meditation and felt fear rise—the fear of running out of money and losing my house and cars.

I'd been out of work for four months and was collecting unemployment. For the first time in my life, I had no significant form of income, and the bills continued to arrive. Fear rose in me that I'd never experienced before.

My savings account was bleeding; my retirement account was next. I believed that I'd die if my bank account hit zero. In fact, I felt close to death because I felt so out of control.

As I sat in easy pose, many thoughts popped into my head. My dad. My mom. My wife and kids. Death. Bankruptcy. Failure. Me on a street corner begging for change. Penniless. My kids hating me. More abandonment.

Meanwhile, I actually possessed plenty of reserves in the form of investments that would cover years of future expenses. I was trapped in scarcity—a feeling I'd run from my entire life. No amount of money made that feeling go away. Prosperity is an emotional state, not a number in a bank account. Prosperity is an emotional state you can hold, regardless of what you have or own.

I did something different this time. I felt into my fear and investigated why, with all of my back-up resources, I felt scarcity. I was more prosperous than the average human and, mentally, I knew that. But I couldn't *feel* it, so the fear and scarcity took hold of me.

I traced my scarcity belief back to what my father taught me—that making money was hard. I traced my survival feelings to my parent's beliefs that "the man" would steal from you, that he'd take what you needed to survive. I traced my need for external love to the loneliness and neglect I'd felt from my mother while she was in her addiction, and the abandonment I felt from my father when my niece was born. I'd been abandoned or turned on by every good friend I'd ever had, so I'd learned to expect neglect, rejection, and abandonment from everyone else.

There are only two innate fears with which you're born: the fear of falling and the fear of loud noises. All other fears are conditioned and, thus, can be unconditioned. Here's how it works:

1. Experiences create beliefs.

2. Beliefs create emotions and feelings.

3. Emotions and feelings create thoughts.

4. Thoughts create action or inaction.

5. Consistent action or inaction creates habits.

6. Habits create character.

7. Character creates outcomes.

8. Outcomes either reinforce or modify our beliefs.

What I experienced and the beliefs I adopted as a child set me up for a painful chase for love, acceptance, and security. Your beliefs create your reality, and when you change your beliefs, your reality changes.

It's actually brain science. The Reticular Activation System (RAS) is a system in your brain that allows you to see only what you believe exists. According to Dr. Bruce Lipton, the subconscious mind processes twenty million bits of data per second, while the conscious mind processes forty bits per second. You decide which forty bits you see based on your beliefs. Your beliefs create your reality.

The RAS filters out everything it's not programmed to see, so you can focus on the few things you expect to see. Have you ever bought a car, then when you drive off the lot, you saw that make and model everywhere? That's the RAS helping you filter what you chose to see. It allows you to see what you decide to see. You get to choose. Want to see pain? You'll see pain. Want to see supportive experiences? You'll see them everywhere. It takes meditation and repetitive focus to tune your brain to experience what you want to see.

My thoughts, feelings, and emotions came from my beliefs, and my beliefs were poisonous. I built a healthy meditation practice so that I could get into a theta brain state, which is how you can access the subconscious mind. By *feeling into* or feeling what I expected to feel, I built new beliefs through visualization.

Dr. Joe Dispenza, one of my favorite spiritual mentors, wrote about how we can rewire our brains to build new beliefs and patterns. And through this new rewiring, you can "remind" yourself of who you are. You can find his work in his bestsellers, and my favorites are *Breaking the Habit of Being Yourself: How to Lose Your Mind and Create a New One* and *You Are the Placebo: Making Your Mind Matter.* This is the process that worked for me.

From childhood, I'd been wired to feel scarcity regardless of the resources I possessed; a lack of love regardless of the love that was in my life; vulnerability regardless of my strength; and inadequacy regardless of the depth of my talents and outcomes. I traced my pain to being abandoned, rejected, neglected, bullied, and feeling like a failure as a child. When I finally became aware of what was driving me to have painful experiences and outcomes in my life, I was able to shift my belief system and see what I wanted to see rather than what I once believed existed. I unraveled who *I thought I was* so I could experience *who I actually was under all of that pain.*

Happiness has nothing to do with who you might become; it comes from appreciating who you are right now. You have a body to move and feel. You have a mind to solve immediate problems. You're a soul who is infinite, eternal, powerful, and abundant. Your body will turn to dust, and your mind will cease to operate. But your soul lives forever. There's nothing to fear. The outcome is guaranteed. When you unravel the pain you've experienced, you can learn who you really are and stop believing in the persona you've created. You stop being the imposter in charge.

> When you unravel the pain you've experienced, you can learn who you really are and stop believing in the persona you've created. You stop being the imposter in charge.

———

I stood ready to give the presentation that I'd prepared. On the screen behind me, looming large was my logo and the words "Creating Powerful Outcomes."

"How many of you think that making money is hard?" I asked to a room full of real estate agents.

About half of the people in the room raised their hands.

"How many of you think that making money is easy?" I asked to show contrast.

The other half of the room raised their hands.

I talked about how beliefs create outcomes and that it's your beliefs that create your outcomes—and everything else you experience in your life. Change your beliefs, change your outcomes. Change the outcomes, change your life.

As your beliefs shift from pain to purpose, your emotions, thoughts, actions, habits, character, and outcomes will shift without effort. On one hand, some people seek to sedate their thoughts and feelings. On the other hand, people who seek peace and happiness understand that their emotions and thoughts expose their deeply held beliefs, and the more you experience life, the more you feel, and the more you feel, the more you heal. Emotional courage means willfully accepting all your emotions, rather than numbing them. There's a difference.

You're a soul who has a body and a mind that transports your soul through this earthly experience. Danger is physical, while fear is a mental and emotional reaction to potential danger. To keep you safe, your body and mind are always on the lookout for danger, and they can even convince you that there's danger when none exists. When the risk of physical death is real, the danger is real, but fear tries to convince you that there's the potential for death in every new, unfamiliar experience. The antidote is to combat this through meditation by becoming aware of and observing the false threats that your thoughts, feelings, and beliefs send your way.

Most leaders who live with imposter syndrome want freedom from their fears, doubts, and pain. Feeling these things, rather than avoiding them, is the best way to get past them.

Most leaders who live with imposter syndrome want freedom from their fears, doubts, and pain. Feeling these things, rather than avoiding them, is the best way to get past them. Leaning into your fears, doubts, and pain allows you to discover their source, and when you know the source, there's an opportunity to heal. To liberate yourself, find the freedom *in* your fears, doubts, and pain, not freedom *from* them.

Align Your Talents and Desires

"Is there any situation where violence is appropriate?" I asked a networking group.

"No!" Two people in the back of the room, a man and a woman, shouted in unison as the other members of the group remained quiet.

"No?" I asked as I walked closer to engage them in a fun conversation.

"I don't think there is," said the man. The woman nodded in agreement.

"Interesting!" I said. "Do you have children?" I asked the man.

"A boy and a girl," he responded with a dad's pride.

I thought for a second. "Is she your wife?" I asked as I pointed toward the female who responded. I smiled and hoped for a yes.

"No," he said with a schoolhouse chuckle. "We're not together."

"Two kids. A burglar breaks into your house, heads upstairs, and prepares to go into your kid's room. What do you do?" I asked, already confident in his response.

He knew he was beaten. "Whatever it takes," he responded.

"Anything?" I asked.

"Anything," he assured me. He turned red from the thought of his children in harm's way.

"How does it make you feel to think of your kids being threatened?" I questioned.

He took a breath as his face reddened even more. "It pisses me off."

"Like angry?" I asked.

"More than angry," he said.

I replied with little hesitation, "So the anger, that emotion that is welled up in you right now, the aggression that's brewing, if your kids were in danger, could that anger and emotion serve you? Does that aggression help you keep them safe?"

"Sure," he said, still emotional about his kids.

"Is there any place for violence?" I asked again.

"Yes," he changed his mind. "There's a place for violence."

All emotion is healthy. People heal by feeling their guilt, shame, fear, and anger. What you feel heals. What you resist persists. All emotions serve. You must feel all your emotions to understand your humanity.

I use aggression and intensity to shift people's beliefs and their positions to serve them. I once used that aggression to create harm. When you understand and use all of your emotions, talents, strengths, and desires in service of others, you can show up in a pure state of love and authenticity.

After you gain some sense of yourself and understand how your past impacts your perception of your current and future states, new opportunities will open up that you once thought were unavailable. When you live in a state of fear and play small, the opportunity to serve a purpose might seem like an impossibility. Because of your doubts and fears, you might live in a state of survival.

As awareness grows and you reach a state of self-acceptance, you start to want opportunities that are aligned with your talents, strengths, and gifts. Since self-appreciation increases, you start feeling that you deserve better than sacrificing yourself for the illusion of safety and security. When you live in a state of sacrifice because you can't see that something better exists, you can't get out of your own way. It's impossible to see the picture from inside the frame.

I once saw a powerful speaker who stated that each day he could do one hundred things, but he chose to do only one that he loved and was passionate about. After he decided to focus on that one thing, he raised his prices because, with a singular focus, the quality of that one thing went way up and word-of-mouth demand increased. When you live in your zone of genius, your personal power grows.

If you look back at your accomplishments, you'll find common threads that run through all them. You'll begin to find your genius. What part did you play in these accomplishments? What talents and strengths did you leverage? What have other people recognized in you that feels natural? What things can you do that feel effortless? What do you love that motivates you and creates energy?

If you continue to explore all of your accomplishments and seek feedback from people you trust, you'll find your zone of genius. When you stay in your zone of genius, and you commit to doing only things that bring you joy, you'll never work again.

Most people get scared at this point because they think work is supposed to be hard. After all, people pay for sacrifice, right? Not so. People pay for passion and excellence. The more I do what I love, the more confidence I gain, and the more I can raise what I charge for those services. People don't pay for sacrifice. People choose to work with people who are energetic, confident, and who create excellent outcomes.

———

Brett is a world-traveled Johnson & Wales Culinary Institute graduate and a sports nutritionist who has cooked for the Denver Broncos, Sacramento Kings, Oregon Ducks, U.S. Women's Olympic Soccer Team, and U.S. Men's and Women's Ski and Snowboard Team at the Olympic games in Korea. He's great at his craft. He's world class.

Brett is an energetic, optimistic, magnetic, charismatic chef in his late twenties, and we started working together when he began his recovery from alcoholism. He wanted support in his recovery and didn't want to go back to a typical restaurant kitchen. Instead, he wanted to start his own service business and leverage his experience.

So I asked Brett what he did well. He believed he was an average chef and somewhat insignificant, even though he'd graduated—on a full-ride scholarship—from one of the best culinary schools in the world and had cooked for some of the top athletes in sports. He was unaware of the power of his talents.

Together, we explored his fears, doubts, and past challenges, and pinpointed how his past had caused him to believe that he wasn't exceptional in any way. He couldn't feel the power of his accomplishments. He'd sedated his doubts and fears. During his career, he'd accumulated numerous testimonials from satisfied customers, and I knew the strength and promise of this young culinary genius. But Brett doubted his own abilities and was unclear about what step to take next.

"What do people say about your food, Brett?" I asked.

"They say it's amazing. But I don't think it is. It's average," he responded with low energy.

"How is it average?" I continued.

Brett thought about my question for a few seconds and said, "Because there are much better chefs in the world."

"I understand. There's always someone better than you, and someone not as good as you. Always," I offered. "Am I a good coach?" I asked. "Have I helped you?"

"Yes!" he said without hesitation.

"There are better coaches in the world, brother. Compared to those coaches on the big stage, who sell books and make millions, I'm average," I said to prove my point. "But you say I'm a good coach. Could that be because I compare myself to the greats while you don't compare me to anyone? Could it be that you're that great, but you compare yourself to those you see as better?"

"Maybe I am," he said.

"Maybe you could listen and honor the people who pour the kind of praise on you that you pour on me."

Over the next seven months, Brett realized that his clients were right. Even in his twenties, he knew everything imaginable about how to select produce and integrate ingredients that will maintain top performance in even the most athletic people. These are specialties of Brett's, but based on his personality and charisma, Brett's zone of genius is teaching. He could talk with people for hours about how to treat delicious and nutritious food as fuel, not feelings.

We narrowed down who he wanted to teach, what he wanted to teach them, and what pain they would avoid with their work.

I asked Brett what he wanted to help athletes accomplish in their lives.

"I love working with athletes," he said. "I feel most connected to those who have no idea how to fuel their bodies and need to rely on other experts for daily guidance. I want to help them have a smooth landing in their retirement and life after sports. They have multiple challenges with nutrition, such as setting up and organizing a kitchen, selecting food, and cooking," Brett said with confidence and courage.

We created an introduction statement he could use when talking to others: "Retired athletes hire me to coach, teach, and help them incorporate real food and performance-level nutrition into their lifestyle." With some newfound courage, Brett began to share this introduction with his friends, family, and even strangers he'd meet in public.

Brett has landed in the kitchens of retired athletes and has helped them organize their kitchens, taught them how to cook, stocked their refrigerators, and turned on his charismatic charm while being the chef for their social engagements. Because of his talents and strengths in the kitchen and his magnetic personality, he's been referred out by many of his clients. His business increases each week, and he now sees the world with a new set of eyes, his challenges with alcohol in the distant rearview mirror.

Since our work together, Brett launched Fuel Good Foods, which creates nourishing food and a line of nutritionally dense granola that supports the nutritional needs of an athletic and active lifestyle. He's also traveled to the University of Richmond to work with the Spiders basketball team to bring world-class nutrition to that program. He's even worked in Utah with the Canadian Ski and Snowboard Team.

Like others with imposter syndrome, Brett never felt that he could create financial success by following his deepest desires and doing what he enjoyed the most. His dream is his job. His job is his mission. And he lives his mission every day.

What you enjoy most is what differentiates you from others, creates exceptional results, and allows your passion, excitement, and genius to shine through. When you gain the confidence, courage, and clarity to focus on what you love, opportunities appear that allow you to live an aligned, prosperous life. The universe wants to support you. It takes a commitment to do what you enjoy and what you do well. Never estimate the true power of your own desires. They are your destiny. Fully embrace every desire you have without guilt or shame.

Cast an Aligned Vision

"What do you want from life?" I asked my client, Lisa.

"What do you mean?" she responded, a puzzled look on her face.

I paused and collected my thoughts. "Fast forward twenty years. What does your business look like? What does your relationship with your significant other look like? What are your hobbies? What does your health look like? What does your financial state look like?"

She looked shocked, and then a slow, amazed look spread across her face, "I know what I want from my business. That's clear. But I have no idea what I want in those other areas."

"Do you use your business to distract you from those other areas?" I asked.

"I must," she acknowledged.

The phone conversation paused. She considered the question more.

"What does your relationship look like now?" I asked.

"Shitty," she responded with sharpness.

"How about your health?" I continued.

"Shitty."

"Fun and enjoyment?" I asked.

"What fun and enjoyment?" she said with a chuckle.

Another pause interrupted the rapid-fire questions. "Lisa, do you have a business plan that creates a plan and some targets?"

"I do," she responded.

"What if you created a plan for everything else in your life that also expresses your vision and some targets?" I said to drive the conversation and offer a new perspective.

About an hour later, I received a message from Lisa that read, "I have no idea what I want in my life other than my business."

"Maybe that's why everything else is shitty," I answered.

————

What you focus on grows. Think about what you want instead of what you don't want. Your thoughts become things. Your prayers are already answered.

This key teaching has been around for millennia, ever since recorded history. What you intend, you create. When you hold something in your mind long enough, with enough faith, and take deliberate action toward it, it will manifest. So, why do you continue to approach life without intention or a vision?

Before I had confidence in myself, it felt impossible to have a purpose and commit to a direction. As I developed confidence and courage, clarity of purpose sprung from the new fertile soil of my mind. With confidence, courage, and clarity, I could take aligned steps forward, but it wasn't until I developed a vision for my life that I saw my life progress in a meaningful, purposeful way. An intentional vision for my life became key to my growth.

One of my clients, Bryan Schroeder, has a real estate investment business called Fasterhouse. When I met Bryan, I noticed he had a relaxed, almost surrendered approach to life and business. Bryan had invested hundreds of thousands of dollars into personal development, and his multi-million-dollar business and the team of superstars he assembled was a testament to that investment.

Bryan developed a vision for what he wanted, updated it when required, and holds that vision in his mind with faith until it unfolds—and it does. God, the universe, source energy—whatever you call the divine—guides us toward our vision when we hold it with clarity. Our vision is a manifestation of a state of universal consciousness that is guided by the divine. Our desires are God's desires. It makes sense that that which is divinely guided will come into manifestation, right?

Bryan's philosophy is simple. Develop a vision, hold that vision in your mind whether things look like they're progressing toward it or not, and that vision—or something better—will show up. Our human minds naturally struggle to hold a vision of perfection when challenges arise, and we give up too soon. Challenges occur to make sure we're clear that we actually want what we say we want.

At his Real Estate Investment Association (REIA), Bryan delivered a presentation that detailed what his vision for his life and business did to create his outcomes. On a cold, windy, Midwest night, in front of a packed crowd of over one hundred real estate investors, Bryan began.

"In the down market of 2008, I found myself with around fifty rental units, and twenty of them were vacant. I'd built my life and business on the foundation that I would earn passive income from my rental portfolio, and now I carried loans for two-fifths of my houses—but they were vacant and weren't generating any income. I couldn't see how my business would survive, how I'd fund the loans, or even where my next source of income would come from or when it would arrive. The entire market was turbulent as we headed into the worst financial disaster in decades."

Bryan continued, "When the real estate bubble burst, I lost tenant after tenant. I'd grown my rental portfolio too quickly and hadn't vetted the initial wave of tenants properly, so I struggled to generate enough rental income to pay for the overall debt. Parts of my vision moved backward. My business partner and I focused on the next activity that could free up some cash."

Bryan talked about what he'd learned about the power of vision in all his self-development. Vision gave him the ability to maintain the course while he navigated the turbulence. That vision was to own 150 free-and-clear, 100 percent filled rental houses. By 2008, he'd built his portfolio to fifty houses, but they weren't yet free-and-clear of debt.

"The way through the chaos," he continued, "wasn't through desperate action, but intentional actions we took while we held the vision of one hundred fifty free-and-clear rentals in our minds. Any time anything unfavorable happened in our business, I brought to mind that vision of financial freedom and 150 free-and-clear rentals, took the next step toward that goal regardless of how much sense it seemed to make, and then we'd take the next step after that," he told the crowd.

"I recognized that when someone stole material from a vacant unit—an air conditioner, copper pipe, or anything else of value—and I focused on the harmful business impact of the event, another similar event happened soon after. So every time something unfavorable happened, I brought to mind the vision of 150 free-and-clear rentals units, and favorable outcomes appeared from nowhere."

What you focus on grows isn't just a cool quote. It's an age-old, time-tested philosophy that has proven itself throughout the ages.

Today, Bryan has 125 rental units with debt loads that are shrinking every month. We estimate that he will own 150 rentals outright by 2022. When the weather allows, he and I sit on a bench outside of his office every Friday and discuss the state of the business, his strategy, the personnel, his leadership development, or any other topic of interest that arises. My time with him is one of my favorite sessions of the week.

Bryan keeps his vision close to him at all times. He often pulls it up on his phone because he has an evergreen document accessible in seconds, so he can make changes as his vision becomes clearer, his mind changes, or his confidence shifts in an area of the business. He's reached a point where his life is fun, and his business is a hobby that feeds his humble but prosperous lifestyle. He continues to attend many self-development seminars, retreats, and classes, and he has multiple coaches.

Bryan's vision is his life's plan, but he isn't attached to the vision to generate happiness. His happiness comes from the next activity on his calendar or in his life. His vision guides all his planned activities and decisions. When he focuses on what he wants instead of what he doesn't want, he gets what he wants. That's why he needs nothing.

———

Over 90 percent of the population lives without an overall vision for their lives. Without a documented vision, you don't have an ultimate plan to compare your major decisions against, such as career moves, investments, financial spends, health activities, hobbies, vacations, etc. When you don't have a firm vision, you might make emotional decisions or live in a state of reaction and chaos. When you have a vision for your life, life slows down so that you can manage day-to-day activities and put yourself in a position to respond, rather than react. Days become less chaotic. Life becomes more fun.

Angie and I developed separate visions, and then we designed a unified vision for our life together. When we were both clear on our visions, the next actions became clear, and we could make hour-by-hour decisions that were aligned with our long-term goals. We now have a combined vision for our life. Our vision includes our health goals. Because of our health goals, when each of us takes time to exercise, the other is never surprised. Because of our vision, we understand what the other is driving toward, and we understand the time it will take to reach those goals.

Every morning we have coffee together, and we make decisions during our coffee time. Sometimes we work while we have coffee, but at a minimum, we carve out space and share the time and the experience together. We've grown together because we planned together. We bounce all of our major decisions against our vision. Our life isn't haphazard. We moved from chaos and reaction to responding to life's circumstances from a position of strength and power.

Executive leaders who are under the spell of imposter syndrome often have no clear plan for their lives. Your life unfolds out of fear that you're not in control, and that is why you're not in control.

Executive leaders who are under the spell of imposter syndrome often have no clear plan for their lives. Your life unfolds out of fear that you're not in control, and that is why you're not in control. You've given away the power over your life and simply hope for the best. When you take back your power and create a comprehensive vision for your life, you can assume your own authority and impact the direction of your life. You're much more powerful than you can ever imagine. When your life unfolds in a way that's in alignment with your vision, it strengthens you because you finally understand how powerful you are. You're significant. You're at the center of everything and critical to everything.

Chapter 5 Work

Are You Showing Up For Yourself?

1. How do you allow yourself to fully embrace and accept all of your pain, suffering, and trauma as stepping stones to your ability to grow and experience the very best in life?

2. How do you allow yourself to feel every emotion?

3. Do you get to show up in your job as you, with all of your talents, gifts, and the natural expression of the best of you on full display?

4. What is your vision that includes all aspects of your life?

Try This!

1. Sit in easy pose. Bring a specific painful memory to the surface. Feel as much of the pain and suffering from that experience as you can handle. Allow it to consume your body. You might not be able to handle a lot at first, but name the energy you feel, and allow it to invite healing. Repeat. With each session, more healing takes place, and more emotional courage builds.

2. The next time you're confronted with guilt or shame, don't shut down. Allow yourself to feel it, noticing that the emotion can't hurt you. Suppression, repression, or escape when you feel the emotion will cause pain. What you resist persists. When you feel a painful emotion and run from it, know that it's trapped and causing you damage whether you try to ignore it or not.

3. Get clear about what your perfect day would look like. Dare to dream. What time would you wake up? How would you spend your day? What hobbies would you have? How would you serve people? What problem would you love to solve for people? What would you do if money weren't an issue? Get clear about your vision and consider the disconnect between your current state and your vision. What can you do right now to close the gap? Start with a single step. Build from there. By recognizing a single step, you begin to attract more alignment. Dare to dream.

Fears.

You were born with two fears.

All your other fears are outcomes of conditioning...

Fear of judgment.

Fear of failing.

Fear of success.

Fear of being inadequate.

Fear of abandonment.

You learned these fears.

And now your brain uses them to keep you "safe."

Your brain keeps you stagnant.

These fears are all bullshit lies that your subconscious
    mind has wired itself to believe are true.

You act from your subconscious mind 95 percent or more
    of the time you're alive.

That means you're acting on bullshit fears over 95
    percent of the time you're awake.

Same for anxiety, depression, addiction, panic, and many
    other mental and emotional imbalances.

All bullshit wiring held in your subconscious mind.

All false and artificial.

Products of your conditioning.

Wanna hear the good news?

You can access and rewrite the programming in your
    subconscious mind.

You don't need to live as you always have as a product of
    your conditioning.

You're in full control... if you desire to improve your
    well-being.

Some will fight to hold onto their victimhood....

And they try to get me to understand that they're not in
    control.

No need.

You can have your condition, behavior, or malaise if you
    want to keep it.

I won't fight you for it.
The truth is that you're in control...
If you want it.
I've learned how.
I've done it myself, and I've taught others to find a
    better life.
You can find one, too.
If you desire.

CHAPTER 6

YOU BELONG.

The alarm went off at 4:30 a.m. I woke up on the floor. I replayed the night before, but it wasn't clear what happened. I tasted booze and felt cotton mouth. I was hungover again.

"Did I hurt anyone?" I thought to myself. "Did I hurt Angie or my girls? Did I drive drunk? Did I get into an accident? Is Angie in bed? Are my girls in their rooms?"

I got up and lost my balance, still intoxicated. I stumbled to Angie's side of the bed, and she wasn't there. I walked into my girls' rooms, peeked in, and they were still in bed. I breathed a sigh of relief. I listened for their breath, and I could hear that they were alive. More relief.

I walked downstairs and looked on the couch in the living room. No Angie. I wasn't sure where she was. I walked into the sitting room, and she was on the couch under covers and pillows that weren't there yesterday. I knew something big had happened.

I moved the shower handle between hot and cold to wake up and sober up. I knew it would be a long day because the fatigue and pain were deep in my bones.

I left while my family still slept.

"Mike, you look like shit," said Jim Kelly, my boss at Stanley Black & Decker when he saw me that morning.

"Rough night, Jim. Angie's sick again, and I was up all night with her," I said, trying to get some pity and sympathy and to deflect at the same time.

"Well, you might split early and go get some rest," he said. Either my lie worked, or he hid it well.

I'd always tried to be the hero to compensate for my low self-worth and rock-bottom self-esteem. In the Marine Corps, we said it takes ten atta-boys to make up for one aw-shit. I tried to play hero as much as I could and hoped that I could cash in those chips when things went south.

"Can't leave early today," I said. "I've got a quality audit, and I can't eject from it."

My cell phone rang. I said goodbye to Jim and stepped out of his office to take the call. In a calmer than expected tone, Angie said, "Do you have any idea what happened last night?"

"None," I said.

"You don't remember our fight? That you pushed me out of the bedroom in front of the girls?" she asked.

Full of regret, I replied, "I don't."

"Mike, the girls saw it all. You blew up out of nowhere. We were all having fun, and you exploded. We all tried to calm you down," she said.

Then there was a long pause on both ends.

"We've got a lot to talk about when you get home," Angie said, serious and stern.

James, my manufacturing engineer, caught me in the hallway while I heard about the damage I'd caused at home. James was always unemotional, so when he approached me, I didn't know if he had good news or bad news. I got off the phone with Angie and felt the full force of my guilt, shame, and hopelessness.

"Neil in shipping fell hard and is on the way to the hospital," James said.

With eyes wide open, I asked, "Is he all right?"

"It was bad, Mike. Looks like his hip gave out while he pulled a pallet jack." James was professional, never exaggerated, and never panicked. This time, his words and tone revealed the severity of Neil's injury.

Neil was a seventy-two-year-old man who'd been with the company for decades. He was also a two-time survivor of cancer, was frail and weak—and a workhorse. Neil never took a break, out-worked everyone else, and often told me that I'd find him dead on the plant floor one day.

As I walked to speak with Emily, my HR partner, I was stopped again, this time by my safety manager. I told her we should both head to Emily's office and discuss Neil's fall. Just then, I got a text from my youngest daughter. "Why did you hurt Mom?"

A wave of emotion and sadness poured through my entire body as I pictured my eight-year-old Meagan, flip phone in her tiny hand. Tears pooled in my eyes.

"I'm sorry," I typed back to her. That's all I could say. I didn't just feel shame, guilt, and pain, I'd become shame, guilt, and pain.

When I got home that night, Angie and the girls were eating dinner. I had dreaded facing them all day. I slowly walked to the table and gave each of them a kiss on the forehead and a gentle hug.

"I'm sorry," I said.

"That's okay, Dad," Katie and Meagan said in their innocent voices. I could still see the pain—the fear—on their faces, but unfortunately, those looks had become normal. I looked at Angie and repeated, "I'm sorry, Angie."

"That's okay," she answered.

I told them it wouldn't happen again, but we all knew it would. In fact, it happened many times in many different ways. In fact, it went on for many more years.

———

A few years later, I left Stanley Black & Decker and pursued a professional opportunity in Saint Louis with SunCoke Energy. After a few months, I settled in and established a clear routine. I arrived at the office near 6:30 a.m., grabbed a cup of coffee, and scanned some emails. I had a regular team meeting at 7:00 a.m., where the off-going supervisor would brief the team on the previous evening.

This morning was different. When I sat down at 6:35 a.m., a head peeked in my office.

"Good morning, Mike," said my boss, Don, a distressed look on his face. "Boiler number two went down about fifty minutes ago."

"Are you fucking kidding me?" I said in an exasperated tone. I leaned back in my chair back and placed my hands on my head. A heat-recovery boiler is a structure that turns heat into steam. When a boiler went down, every hour we lost millions of dollars in energy production. A boiler down meant little rest for the week ahead, just like the past week when a different boiler was down.

"Yup," he said. "What time did you leave last night?"

"Boiler number four was back online this morning at 2:30, and I got home at around 3:30." I was dog-tired and couldn't believe another boiler had disrupted my work life.

"Another fun day at SunCoke Energy." Don grinned.

I'd left Stanley Black & Decker to escape. I'd wanted more money, power, and authority, and I'd gotten all of them. I was now the operations manager, responsible for wall-to-wall operations of a $350MM operation. The general manager was my boss, and he was the conduit between me and corporate headquarters in Lisle, Illinois.

My first day as the operations manager, I said to Janet, the HR manager, as I was filling out my new-hire paperwork, "This job is perfect, and I'm excited to get started."

Janet looked at me with a sideways grin, and with a smooth Kentucky accent, almost whispered, "Yeah, just wait. You're the third operations manager in three years. Keep that excitement level as long as you can."

Don left after he told me about the new boiler outage, and I dressed in the heavy, flame-retardant uniform I wore while in the plant. Then I began my death march to the boiler and thought about the easier position I'd left at Stanley Black & Decker. I started to think about my next job, too. I wanted something different to escape the pressure and stress. I felt inadequate, ill-prepared, and like a sacrificial lamb served up on a platter.

"Keep that excitement level as long as you can," bounced around in my head again. The excitement was over.

Whether it was the Marine Corps, Tektronix, Stanley Black & Decker, SunCoke, or Kemlab Production Components, every day I felt the need to run away. So much came at me at all times that I couldn't sort the priorities from the noise. I couldn't be present from minute-to-minute, and instead, lived in a constant state of overwhelm, compounded by the fact that the operational tempo was high, my responsibilities were immense, and my feelings of inadequacy were in full force at all times.

There were days I called in and "worked from home." There were days when my hangover was so painful that I couldn't move, and there were days when I felt emotionally paralyzed. I wanted to escape. Before I began my self-mastery journey, there wasn't one day that I felt that my life was together, fulfilling, or that I wouldn't crash and burn. Chaos was my life. I woke up, fought the next battle, the next crisis, and anticipated the next catastrophe. Most days, I didn't want to live.

Near the end of my time in corporate America, I had no personal power, my family was a disaster, and my job performance inadequate. I was living in a house of cards that could fall apart any day, at any time. I tried many different tactics to get relief. I set priorities, scheduled my day, and planned every move, and all those great plans unraveled as soon as the chaos of the day slammed into me.

The issue was never actually the events of the day. My internal state was chaotic, so the events triggered and caused more pain inside my already chaotic mental and emotional state.

When executive leaders carry the imposter syndrome, it feels impossible to make sense out of the chaos. There's no clarity. You try to gain control only to have the next event unravel your plans. Since you feel inadequate, you never get a firm grip on your life. You give your power away, and you only stand a chance to regain that power by committing to reestablish your own significance and well-being in your body, mind, and emotions. Your soul recognizes its worth and value. The gap between what your soul knows and what your body, mind, and emotions recognize is the suffering.

Your soul recognizes its worth and value. The gap between what your soul knows and what your body, mind, and emotions recognize is the suffering.

This chapter will address three primary drivers of overwhelm: lack of presence; the inability to understand fear, anxiety, worry, and concern that create self-doubt; and the inability to understand the talents and strengths we can call on each day. The professional who masters these can feel focused, powerful, and capable.

Remain Present

My mind was in a constant firestorm at all times. I felt that life moved faster than I could respond, so I reacted every second. The difference between a response and reaction is in the proactive ownership of your circumstances. Reaction in a key results area keeps you in a desperate state of catch-up and mismanagement. I was rewarded for solid performance, but day-to-day felt like pure chaos. I never outran the feeling of chaos until the chaos brought me to my knees.

Once I was relieved of my responsibilities from corporate America, I found myself in a different type of chaos. I didn't know how to put my life back together. My thoughts and emotions were like a machine gun firing a never-ending belt of rounds.

Do we have enough food to eat?
How will I fund Christmas?
I want a beer.
What if an appliance goes out?
I have a half tank of gas; how long can I make that last?
My girls think I'm a failure.
I hope Angie sleeps all day.
I want a beer.
Why did I let this happen?

How did I let this happen?
I'm a failure.
How will I fund Christmas?
We're going to lose our house.
The girls love this house. It's going to be foreclosed.
They'll hate me.
I hate me.
I want a beer.
Do we have enough food to eat?

I couldn't get my feet under me. My self-talk was critical. This combination created mental pressure, self-hatred, and damage to my well-being. Before and after my terminations, my focus was non-existent; I couldn't even write a priority list that made sense. When I did write a priority list, my next hundred thoughts during the next minute made that list obsolete.

When I lost my source of income, the mental pressure increased. I had to keep the Kitko corporate ship afloat—not a corporate enterprise I didn't own. The stress was unbearable.

————

Paul asked me to perform three mini-meditations, or mind-breaks, per day. I only did this out of compliance, but they changed my life.

"Let's discuss mind-breaks. Download the Insight Timer app on your phone. Set the warm-up period for forty-five seconds and the duration for three minutes. When you hear the bell, count your exhales. Do this exercise four times per day, and whenever you feel the mental pressure increase, pause and take a mind-break," Paul coached me.

"That's meditation! I'm not meditating!" I said aggressively.

"You can either do the same things and get the same results or try some different things and get different results," he said, not attached to my choice.

Meditation held a stigma in my mind as a practice for Buddhists, new-agers, and hippies. I made sure no one at home saw me doing it, so they didn't even know that I meditated. If someone noticed, I'd convinced them that I was just resting my eyes.

For the first few weeks, I performed the mind-breaks out of compliance, more afraid of the stigma than the benefits. I was more concerned about how I looked than what type of peace and mindset shift the activities could help me to discover.

It took a few weeks, but after a while, I found peace inside of my mini-meditations. Soon, the only peace I felt was during my mind-breaks. They became a welcomed activity instead of a forced march. I increased my morning meditation to a half hour, and I craved peace so much that I looked forward to my next meditation as much as I had once looked forward to my next beer.

After a few months of this, I felt grounded and peaceful inside of my meditations, and that peace carried on afterward as well. Soon, I performed three to four mind-breaks a day, and I held space for half-hour meditations two to three times per day. I didn't have much else to devote my time to, so I learned to love my peace, quiet, and stillness.

During a meditation session, when you connect with your body, breath, energy, feelings, emotions, and heartbeat, you focus your mind on those areas in your body. When your mind wanders, you bring your awareness back to your body. You can't focus on your body and your thoughts at the same time, so as you give focused attention to your body, your thoughts slow. Between these thoughts you'll find peace, calm, happiness, joy, and love. It's your thoughts that keep you from feeling the peace that's always present.

We've all been conditioned to rely on left-brain thought. Schools push standardized tests and analytical problem solving, businesses rely on data, and if you can't prove it, you can't believe it. Left-brain thought relies on facts, figures, data, separation, proof, evidence, logic, science, math, and all things concrete and factual.

Right brain thought consists of art, music, beauty, love, unity, compassion, understanding, empathy, belief, and the unseen. When school budgets get cut, the first things to go are art and music, which are right-brained activities. As you condition your children to rely on their left-brain thought, they lose the ability to see the world from the view of trust, faith, and the unseen.

When you meditate for extended periods, your left and right hemispheres merge again. You know what can't be known, see what can't be seen, and understand what's difficult to understand. When you meditate, life slows, and your ability to see things with a clearer lens grows stronger.

The average human has 80,000 to 100,000 thoughts per day. A healthy meditation practice slows the pace and volume of those thoughts and also reduces the volatility in the mind. Some mindfulness teachers have called these thoughts your inner roommate or the inner critic, and when you quiet the mind, the critical roommate quiets.

Meditation enables human beings to experience the world from the joyous perspective of childhood and to once again view things from a less burdensome, less dramatic, more playful perspective. The amazing part is you don't sacrifice left-brain intelligence and intensity; they strengthen as well.

I've reshaped my world-view with this age-old practice that I originally dismissed.

"How do you feel?" Paul asked a few weeks after I began the mind-breaks.

"I do about four mind-breaks a day. I'd stay in that state all day if I could. It's peaceful, and I feel more peaceful and calmer after I finish," I answered.

The process worked. As my thoughts slowed, my peace and contentedness increased. My desire and love for meditation increased. The negative self-talk slowed, so my overall perspective of life improved, and I gained greater clarity and confidence in who I am and what purpose I serve. Meditation isn't just for the woo-woo. Over time, the brain rewires its neuropathways, and peace, calm, joy, and optimism are solidified into your life.

How much should you meditate?

There's a tale of a Buddhist monk who asked his guide, "Teacher, what if I can't find an hour to meditate every day?" His teacher replied, "Then you need two hours." Meditation allows you to center, ground, and create space in your life.

My daughter, Meagan, notices when I don't meditate. One time, she recognized that I was off-balance and asked, "Dad, did you meditate today?" I replied no, then she made me take some time to collect myself, regroup, ground, and create personal power. When you grow a solid meditation practice, you crave a session like you crave food. Meditation is food for your mood and a tool to find presence in the chaos of the day.

Meditation builds mindfulness in the moment, reduces mental chaos and anxiety, and brings peace into your life. This peace enables you to live a more focused, present life and reduces the volatility you experience. You'll move from a weakened state of reaction to a powerful state of response.

When a leader suffers from the imposter syndrome, there's some neglect in total self-care as he or she gives up their personal health and well-being for the good of others. Meditation can be a critical aspect of powerful leadership and will help you take back control of your day and your power. Meditation creates on the inside what social significance creates in our world. Out of all the life changes I've made, if I had to choose just one to continue for the rest of my life, it would be meditation. It's that powerful.

Out of all the life changes I've made, if I had to choose just one to continue for the rest of my life, it would be meditation. It's that powerful.

Identify Your Deepest Fears and Doubts

We're all subconscious creatures of habit. What do you think about when you tie your shoes? It's probably not your shoes. Pay attention next time. When you first learned to tie your shoes, your three- to four-year-old brain held focused intensity. As the process became muscle memory, you stopped focusing and began to think about anything but your shoes. This is your subconscious mind at work. Your subconscious programs drive most of your life.

Your subconscious stores memories from your past experiences all the way back to in utero. Your subconscious also contains programming from past generations. Beliefs and conditioning are passed down from generation to generation as you teach the next generation the painful beliefs and conditioning you learned yourself. Emotionally charged experiences, whether favorable or unfavorable, are stored as programs. Emotional charge creates beliefs. Neutrally charged events pass through without notice.

When you experience fear, doubt, anxiety, worry, and concerns, these can be tracked to a stored memory, program, and emotion connected to an experience. You can gain self-awareness and begin to heal unhealthy programming, but it first takes deep investigation and brutal honesty.

Tony Fonte is a very close friend, and I consider him my brother. Tony hasn't had an easy life. He was raised in an angry, volatile family with lots of money and mounds of religious guilt. He was abused as a child, then became an abusive husband to four wives, neglecting his children from multiple marriages.

When we met in 2016, he'd already healed much of his anger, but he was in financial strain, although he'd earned three different coaching certificates in advance of launching a professional coaching business. He wasn't attracting clients, and he struggled to pay his rent every month.

We went to work to understand where his fears, doubt, anxieties, worries, and concerns originated, so he could heal. Most people avoid this process, but Tony wanted his freedom more than his pain. We identified his feelings and emotions that revolved around worthlessness, guilt, and shame for struggling to provide for his children, and guilt and shame for abusing his four wives.

His issues could be traced back to the messages he received when he was a child, including the idea that people with money are greedy, and they steal from the poor. These beliefs were stored in his subconscious as his belief system. His father had simply passed on to Tony what he'd been taught. He'd done the best he could with what he knew. The toxic emotions and feelings that Tony experienced stemmed from these beliefs.

In 2011, his wife died suddenly, and he was left to raise his youngest child all alone. As he grew a strong relationship with his daughter, he realized that she would marry a man like him—an angry asshole. He decided to make some profound changes.

Tony began a long process to heal the anger that had been inside him since he was a child. That anger fueled manipulation, abuse, neglect, rage, narcissism, violence, and many other unhealthy behaviors. It took Tony years to face himself and heal the monster within.

During the process of introspection and investigation, Tony remembered the physical and verbal abuse from his childhood, which created feelings of unworthiness, money guilt, religious guilt, shame about his abuse, fear of being abandoned, and feeling unloved and unlovable. Tony had no idea how to operate in a healthy emotional manner, so he attacked everyone in his life.

"What's your biggest issue?" I asked him in one of our first sessions.

Tony thought a few minutes and responded, "That I'm not worthy of making money. My dad told me I'd amount to nothing and that I'd never make any money because I was a stupid kid. I've spent forty years proving him right."

"What do you want to believe?" I asked.

"I want to feel worthy. Deserving. I want money to flow easily to me," he said with real tears in his eyes.

"I want you to feel that pain from the past," I said. "I want you to recall the memory of him yelling at you. I want you to feel every bit of emotion in your body and allow it to absorb you completely. Then, after you sit with the feelings and emotions a while, they'll begin to process naturally.

"When you feel like you're done—and you'll know when you are—I want you to conjure up the mental image of making lots of money. Imagine it raining down on you. Feel what that feels like. Bring yourself to feel and experience these beliefs, 'I'm worthy. I deserve wealth. I'm valuable. I easily cover my bills.' Repeat that cycle a few times. Your body and mind will begin to process the old emotions and will start to rewire your brain for these new beliefs. Repeat this every day. Repetition is critical."

Tony was professionally trained but still hadn't experienced the very best release technique known to mankind: feeling the pain to allow it to process. If you can't feel it, you can't heal it. What you resist persists. These are true for every painful emotion buried within, whether you're aware of them or not.

During the process, Tony made many mental shifts, and some of them allowed him to rewire his beliefs to see and feel things in a healthier manner. We moved through his grief over the loss of his wife, anger from the abuse he witnessed, guilt and shame from his own abusive words and action, and the feelings of desperation and anxiety from his feelings of scarcity. As Tony processed each piece, he found peace. Not all of the emotions were released at once; it might take years to fully release the trauma. But as he released the painful energy trapped inside, he felt more and more freedom.

Recently, I saw Tony's name pop up on my phone.

"I got another client today!" he said, excited.

"Awesome! Tell me all about it!" I said.

"He's in my networking group. Knows that I held a lot of anger and asked how I moved past it. I told him I processed the anger and allowed it to heal. He asked how. I told him that I could teach him, and we discussed the terms," Tony said.

"Sounds like it was an easy conversation," I said.

"Effortless. I felt worthy of helping him and deserving of the money he's going to pay me," Tony said.

"That's a big deal, Tony." I felt like a dad watching his kid open Christmas presents.

"Do you realize that I've been trying to coach for four years," he said, "and this is the first time I've ever had two clients at the same time?"

"I didn't, Tony. I didn't. I'm proud of you, brother!" I glowed.

I could hear the emotion in his voice. "I've processed and released more blocks in a few months than I had in four years, and I've worked hard over the years," Tony said through joyful tears.

"I know you have," I responded. "And it's because you face your shit, and your courage is through the roof. Give yourself some credit."

Every now and then, I get calls from Tony about how much more present, grounded, and confident he feels. It's only a matter of time before he breaks out. His story is too powerful to remain small.

———

People think that they've healed from trauma and abuse when they no longer have conscious thoughts about them. But just like driving a car without fully paying attention, your unconscious programs still drive you through life without your conscious awareness. Emotions that are attached to painful memories can persist if you avoid feeling them or spend much of your life sedating and avoiding them.

When you bring a memory to your conscious awareness, try to feel the emotion attached to that memory without attempting to push it away. Your body will process the emotion, and you will heal. This process becomes even more effective during meditation. Your body has everything it needs to heal itself, which includes the buried emotions of past circumstances.

Emotional courage is the courage to feel every emotion, not just the ones that feel good. When you learn to feel and process the painful emotions trapped inside, you see that they can't hurt you. The pain and trapped emotion are harmless unless you allow them to remain trapped.

Leaders who suffer from imposter syndrome hold onto pain and suffering from past traumas and experiences.

When you run from your fears, it's impossible to feel authentic and valuable. Leaders who suffer from imposter syndrome hold onto pain and suffering from past traumas and experiences. When you face the pain and suffering from these experiences, the fears of the future dissolve, and you're free to navigate the present moment and face the future with confidence, courage, and clarity. If you lean into the pain, it will dissolve. You'll find strength when you move toward the pain.

Align Your Talents

Rene was a process engineer at Tektronix, the first company I worked for after I exited the Marine Corps. I was a production line manager, and Rene was my support. He reported to another manager, but he was my support. My first meeting with Rene went like this:

"Hi, Rene, my name is Mike."

"Hi, Mike, what do you need?"

I showed him a drawing I'd sketched. "I need a program, and I'm thinking it looks like so-and-so and does so-and-so, and it's colored blue and red."

Rene stared at me, and in a thick German accent said, "Let's get something clear. I'm an engineer. I'm smarter than you. Give me your problem, and I'll come up with a solution ten times better than anything you could come up with."

I stood there for a second and enjoyed the stare down. The battle lines were drawn.

"Wow. Okay," I said. I dropped the sketch onto his desk and walked away and didn't connect with him for a few weeks. Our relationship started off with a bang.

You might find yourself in the wrong place, with the wrong basic skills, or in the wrong position to execute at the highest level. It's important that when you feel like you're in over your head, you evaluate the requirements of your position and make sure your talents and skills fit. When requirements and talent aren't aligned, you'll struggle.

Rene and I didn't see eye to eye. I was personable, and he was abrasive. Over the next few years, we grew together. We worked on many projects and developed great trust in each other. We became great friends.

After a few years, we both went our separate ways but remained in close contact. I took on the plant manager position at Stanley Black & Decker, and on my first day, I called Rene.

I heard the phone pick up, and a much-thinned-out German accent responded on the other end of the phone. "This is Rene."

"Hey, Rene! Don't get too comfortable there," I said as soon as he picked up.

"Mike?"

"Yup," I said as I stared out of my office window that overlooked the production floor.

"Why?"

"This plant. It needs lots of help, and you're my guy. You're coming with me," I said without a single doubt.

"I'm not changing companies again," he said forcefully, his accent getting thicker with every word.

"We'll see," I said. I smiled and hung up the phone.

I knew it was only a matter of time until I convinced him to make the move. Three months later, he joined me as my operations manager.

―――――

There was a knock on my office door.

"Come in," I said as I signed an expense report for some raw material that exceeded anyone else's financial approval limit.

"Is this how you greet new employees?" Rene said as he peeked his head around the crack in the door.

I stood up and walked to the door and greeted him with an ear-to-ear smile on my face.

I said, "It is when they arrive earlier than our agreed time!" I responded, happy to have my good friend back as my partner and as my operational horsepower.

When Rene took over the Operations Manager and Continuous Improvement Leader position, it was the first time that he'd reported to me. I allowed him to have free reign over operations, and that went south fast.

"Why didn't the order ship? That's unacceptable guys!" Rene said in a dismissive tone, without a grasp of the circumstances that caused the delay.

"We couldn't get the order on the machines," said the cell leader.

"There's no excuse for missing an order like this. None!" Rene scolded the men.

He was also abrasive when he led discussions with some of our production associates. His statements were direct, accusatory, and arrogant. Rene's technical skills were superb, but his leadership lacked the same polish. I received complaint after complaint from team members on the shop floor; some threatened to quit. I cooled everyone down and thought of a new plan.

Rene lacked people skills. I couldn't afford for Rene to make anyone quit. He was in over his head, and I needed him. He was the single most talented individual I'd ever worked with.

I pulled him back a bit from his interactions with the members of the production team. I reassumed leadership on the production walks with the intention of teaching and coaching Rene to help him understand the positive impacts of asking questions for better understanding. I led all the interaction with our production team until Rene could demonstrate improved skills.

"Safety met our goals yesterday," the production cell leader said in a matter-of-fact tone while he pointed to the key performance indicator board behind him.

The management team and I were on our morning production walk through the production cells. Cells were smaller sections of the production process that we measured for performance. As we walked the plant, each cell leader stepped forward and reported on the prior day's performance. This practice drove accountability, alignment, and performance, while it allowed our leaders to lead.

"Quality met our goals," he continued. "Delivery was below the goal."

"What drove the miss, Chuck?" I asked.

Tom looked me in the eyes and responded, "There was an order that missed because we didn't have the inventory."

"How did we miss that?" I asked Chuck in a curious, rather than accusing, tone.

"The order was released to our production area with the assumption that the materials had arrived as scheduled. The delivery date was supposed to be yesterday, but it wasn't delivered," he said.

"Rene, why was the order released without material? Isn't the process to release the orders with the material, so that the cell leaders don't have to manage the orders?" I asked.

Rene responded, "That's the process. I'll review the document, retrain the team, and make sure it doesn't happen again."

I looked at Frank, my materials manager. "Frank, why didn't the material arrive on time?"

"It was held up at the warehouse, and it didn't make it on yesterday's truck," Frank said.

"Did you know the order was released to the cell?" I asked Frank.

Frank replied with integrity, "I did."

"Did you tell Rene and Chuck that the material was delayed?" I asked.

"No," he said.

"We've got a few process breakdowns. Let's review the processes tomorrow and make sure we're all on the same page. We need to make sure we're not wasting Chuck's time and resources. This is a management issue, not a cell performance issue," I concluded.

"Thanks, Chuck. Please continue," I said as I looked at him and nodded my head.

At first, I'd asked Rene to observe my interaction with team members to witness how asking questions always revealed more information. The production team knew their jobs, and they needed some of Rene's problem-solving expertise to fine-tune their performance. When a problem became apparent, I tossed the conversation to Rene, and he demonstrated his problem-solving mastery. Where he struggled was in asking the right questions. After some practice, Rene learned to uncover process issues in a curious, non-aggressive tone.

After a few months of leadership and much coaching, I turned control of the walk back over to Rene, and I stepped out of the way to allow him to shine.

"How'd we do yesterday, Chuck?" Rene asked with confidence and constructive intention. Machines blared on the production floor, the sound of metal cutting metal. It was beautiful to see and hear because when the machines cut metal, we made money.

Chuck pointed to the board: "Safety, good. Quality missed the goal because of a broken tool during the production run."

"How many components did we make with the broken tool?" Rene asked.

Chuck counted again and said, "Ten."

"The machinist is supposed to perform a full quality check between how many of that part?" Rene asked with graceful tact.

"Five. The machinist is to check every fifth part completely. The guy who ran this part didn't follow instructions and received a verbal warning for not following the documented process," Chuck responded.

"Was the machinist trained on the procedure, and did he have access to the document while he ran the parts?" Rene dug further to make sure he'd collected enough information.

Chuck nodded his head in agreement well before he responded, then said, "Yes. I made sure all training and sign-offs were completed."

"Nice job, Chuck. Thanks. Continue." Rene said, proud that the team had followed proper procedures. He didn't ever get belligerent or speak in a condescending tone. Instead, he remained poised, constructive, and professional during the discovery process.

Rene had witnessed the benefit of establishing rapport instead of exerting aggression. He needed to see what "good" looked like. After he saw that less abrasive interactions created healthier outcomes, he adjusted with ease.

———

After I accepted a position with SunCoke Energy, and before my family moved to Saint Louis, I announced that Rene would be the next plant manager for the Stanley Black & Decker plant team. Over a few years, he grew, which allowed his interpersonal skills to sharpen to a level which enabled his success. Sound leadership establishes rapport, builds trust, and extends grace for errors while enforcing consequences where necessary. I had the pleasure of seeing Rene blossom into these qualities.

When I announced Rene's promotion, it was the single most rewarding day of my professional career. I had seen a talented technical professional and watched him develop his leadership skills.

At first, Rene was in over his head. He'd struggled because of culture shock and exposure to new circumstances. If I had let him sink or swim alone, I'd have had to either fire him or hire a new production team. He had some underdeveloped skills, but he adjusted and rose to the challenge.

Driven professionals seek out and accept new challenges. It's a bonus when the opportunity leads to advancement and increased responsibility. It's your responsibility to understand your strengths, non-strengths, and debilitating weakness, and to seek training and coaching where necessary. If you stay rooted in your weaknesses, you may be stuck forever.

Leaders who feel the burden of imposter syndrome are often blind to their own talents. You must become self-aware enough to discern and focus attention on those talents and skills that will move the needle the most. Those stuck in the imposter syndrome are afraid of exposing their weaknesses—and may feel that all their traits are weaknesses. That's why they hide.

It's critical to know yourself. Surround yourself with people who recognize your abilities and who provide safety. These people allow you to be you. If you don't align your talents and have people who help keep you aligned, you'll risk all the progress you've made during your career.

Chapter 6 Work

Are You Showing Up For Yourself?

1. Do you struggle to feel like you belong even though you're successful?

2. Do your mental and emotional states cause you pain? Is your approach to run from fear or to run toward purpose?

3. Are you able to sit still in silence and stillness and find peace and ease in your body, mind, and emotions?

4. Do you struggle to feel in control of your life? Do you *react* or *respond* to circumstances?

Try This!

1. Get in a comfortable resting position. Set a timer on your phone for three minutes. When the timer starts, close your eyes and focus on your breathing. Count your exhales. When you recognize your mind wandering, bring your focus back to your breathing and resume counting. Bring all of your focus to your breathing. Afterward, consider that you can't think and observe your breath at the same time. Repeat three to four times per day, especially when starting a major task.

2. Journal and keep track of all of the fears and doubts that enter your awareness. Do this for a week. What are the common themes? Think back to your childhood. What memories do you recall that could have created the fear? Ask yourself that question for each fear. During meditation, bring the memory to your awareness and allow the fear to surface. Hold the memory and process the stored emotion.

3. Don't think of a purple elephant! Did you think about one? Of course, you did. You can't stop yourself from thinking. Meditate for twenty minutes, focusing on the space between your closed eyes. Notice the thoughts slow as you become aware of your body. Over time, your mental chaos will slow as well. Practice daily.

Happiness.

You need little in this life.
Food, water, shelter from the elements.
The secret to getting everything you desire in life?
Those things that you feel you can't do?
Do them.
Those things you can't live without?
Live without them.
Those things that you must have to be happy?
Don't have them.
And choose happiness anyway.
Bring yourself to realize that you need little in this life.
Feel what it feels like to survive without your ongoing
    illusion of what happiness involves, outside of the
    bare necessities.
Attachment and aversion are poison to your happiness.
Break the bondage of attachment and aversion that we
    allow to strengthen...
And you'll feel what true love and happiness is.
True happiness.
Not the illusion of happiness we create.

CHAPTER 7

CREATE SPACE AND TIME.

"I've got too much to do to take time off."

These words feel like a slow, torturous death to me and represent a *live to work* mindset, not a *fund your life* approach. Life and business can intertwine with seamless perfection if you allow them to. The need to sacrifice your life for income comes from deep-seated emotional issues.

You walk this earth and experience this experience in this lifetime only once, and to spend the largest percentage of your time on activities that are busy-work or are performed out of fear of failure

> **Life and business can intertwine with seamless perfection if you allow them to. The need to sacrifice your life for income comes from deep-seated emotional issues.**

or fear of missing out shows that you have emotional scars that must be exposed and healed.

"So, what time is the first delivery expected?" I asked my operations leader, a drink in my hand beside a pool in Cancun, Mexico. The sun was blaring on my bald head and tan body, while my children splashed in the pool nearby.

I heard my operations leader, Rick, repeat the question, using another phone in his other hand to ask the transportation company what time the first delivery of coal was scheduled that night.

"At 10:00 p.m.," said Rick as he repeated the answer the transportation company had given him.

"That's unacceptable, Rick. They missed our 7:00 p.m. delivery time yesterday, too. What's their phone number? I'll call them myself," I said with anger.

Rick gave me the phone number. He told the person on the other end of the phone that I'd call directly. I said goodbye to Rick, and as soon as I hung up, I dialed the number.

"This is Mike Kitko, the operations manager for SunCoke Energy. What time do you expect the first truck of coal to be delivered tonight?" I asked with a firm tone. I knew the answer and was prepared to attack.

"Hey Mike, this is Dave. We'll be there at 10:00 p.m.," said my counterpart at our transportation company who hauled 120 semi-truckloads of coal each night to my metallurgical coke energy plant in Granite City, Illinois. The coal was baked and created coke, a basic ingredient in steel.

"Dave, you missed delivery yesterday. I lost tens of thousands of dollars. I need the trucks there by 7:00 p.m. per our agreement."

"I don't have the trucks and drivers tonight, Mike," Dave said in a matter of fact tone like that response was enough.

"That's not my problem, Dave. Find drivers and trucks. We have a signed contract that I get my coal at 7:00 p.m. Your trucks and drivers are not my problem. Hire them from somewhere else. I want my coal," I said. I watched my kids play in the pool.

The poolside server took my empty cup and put another drink in my hand. A cerveza with lime. The waitstaff made sure I had a drink in hand with another waiting on the table while I paced the pool, phone in my hand. Angie lounged in a chair and read a book, also with a drink.

There was silence on Dave's end. We'd been through this song and dance before, and Dave knew I didn't appreciate his or his team's performance. Poor performance had become their norm.

"Dave!" I yelled so loudly that the other vacationers overheard. "Your issues are not my issues. Fix them. I want my deliveries on time tonight. If you want me to call another transportation company and hire them and pass the costs on to you, I will. Now, let me know what you want to do, Dave. You want me to call them, or do you want to do it yourself? I want my coal at 7:00 p.m."

Dave was a stubborn guy, but when pressed, he did the right thing. "I'll call them, Mike," he said in a hushed tone.

"Great, Dave. Thanks for your support. I'm by the pool in Mexico. If you have any problems tonight with the delivery, call me. Don't call my guys at the plant; I want you to call me. And when the trucks make the first delivery, I want to hear from you to confirm."

"Roger that, Mike," said Dave, Army vet to the Marine vet.

"Thanks again, Dave," I said as I hung up the phone.

We received our coal on time that evening.

———

I remember when I felt like there was nothing I could do to contribute enough, whether I was at the plant or on my phone from poolside. I worried that if the operation went on without me, then I wasn't necessary and I'd lose my position. I also felt like self-sacrifice was expected.

Leaders who suffer from imposter syndrome often feel their time isn't valuable. Since you place low value on yourself and know you're replaceable, you feel you must be engaged and active—busy—at all times. Imposters give up their happiness out of fear.

Because of deep fear, you try to maintain control of your external environment. You can take back your power when you schedule your life on your own terms and guard that schedule, ask for help often, do what's valuable and ignore the rest, become aware when you've gotten busy out of fear, and learn the value of relaxation time.

Schedule on Your Terms and Guard Your Time

Back then, my days were chaotic, out of control, and I had a hard time saying no. My schedule and calendar were full because I said yes to everything, which created conflicts, a break-neck tempo, and made everything feel urgent. I never felt that I was worthy enough to set boundaries. I often felt like a victim, even though I was the authority figure.

One day, I walked into my office at Stanley Black & Decker with a firm plan for the day. I'd finally decided to take control of my schedule. I sat down at my desk and took out my notebook. I had started and then stopped using that same notebook to create priorities and a plan a hundred times before. I jotted down a list of urgent and important tasks that required my attention, transferred those notes into my electronic calendar and priority list, and hammered out the most urgent and important item.

There was a knock on my office door. The shift had begun fifteen minutes earlier, and machines were cutting metal to make tools. The regular morning meeting ended, and my leadership team and the production staff had some questions.

"Come in," I said.

"Mike, the guys on the production floor have some questions for you," one of my supervisors stated. "Okay, I'll be right there," I said.

I left my desk and exited my office to discuss whatever matter was important to my team.

"Mike, do you have a second?" a machinist asked.

"After you're finished with Dan, can I get a minute of your time, Mike?" another machinist asked with patience and respect.

After I spoke to that member of my team, another shop-floor employee caught me to ask about paychecks. Within seconds, I received a call from my boss, which I took, and he asked some questions and sought an update about a major project I was leading. I stepped away from the employee and went in a different direction to align with my boss. When I answered my boss' question, another team member stood near me as if to form a line for my time.

While I spoke with the employee, I realized I'd missed the start of a meeting that was on my calendar, and a paralyzing cold chill ran down my spine. I was planning to tell the people in the meeting a lie to cover up my ineptitude. I ran to the meeting.

This pattern repeated throughout my career and intensified as the imposter syndrome intensified. I felt I needed to be all things to all people, and I let everyone down in the meantime. I damaged trust over and over with increasing magnitude. I felt like if I ever took ownership of my schedule or if I ever delayed conversations, time requests, or phone calls, people wouldn't appreciate me or have confidence in my abilities.

After my second termination, I altered my days, my habits, and my approach to life. I faced the fact that I was afraid to say no to people, which depleted me and sent me into a spiral. I could only react instead of responding. I felt out of control. This same behavior showed up at work, at home, and in every dimension of my life. How you show up in one area of your life is how you show up in all of them.

When you don't feel worthy of creating space in your life, set your priorities, or own your schedule, you shrink to others. When you shrink in one area of your life, you shrink in all areas.

> **How you show up in one area of your life is how you show up in all of them. When you shrink in one area of your life, you shrink in all areas.**

At first, I allowed new clients to determine the times we met and lengths of our visits. I struggled to say no to any request, even allowing early Sunday morning meetings, which presented family challenges. Over time, I learned to set boundaries and establish limits, which other people honored. I set limits and controls and got my power back without consequence. The consequences I expected had been fear based, not real.

The reason other people didn't honor my schedule, boundaries, and limits was because I didn't. It's always that way. All the respect we receive first comes from self-respect. In the absence of self-respect, external respect will be absent as well.

Even my most powerful and significant clients honor my schedule. They respect me at the level I respect myself—no more and no less. Over time, I learned to have a straight conversation with my clients about my expectations, which allowed me to guard my schedule.

———

"Let's set a recurring time to meet," I said to my new five-figure client at the beginning of our full-day intensive coaching session. He'd flown in from Atlanta to meet with me on the first Sunday of our coaching agreement.

"I can meet on Thursday afternoons," he replied.

"I schedule repeat coaching sessions on Tuesdays, Wednesdays, and Fridays," I said. I have various times open on those days. Can I send you a link to my calendar, and you can see what works best for you?" I asked.

"Of course," he agreed.

"I sent it to your email. Open it now, and let's settle on a time," I said.

He opened his email, clicked on my calendar link, and said, "How about Wednesdays between three and four?"

"Perfect!" I replied. Let's lock that in. For the next six months, we'll meet every Wednesday between three and four Central time. You'll have vacation weeks, and I'll have vacation weeks. We'll play it by ear on those weeks, and we'll schedule a brief call if need be. But if not, we'll skip those weeks."

"Sounds good," he said with a nod and a smile.

When I think back to my days in corporate life, some people guarded their schedule, and everyone honored the boundaries they put in place. I learned who was more flexible than others. I worked around them with respect and learned to trust their intent. I was jealous. As Stephen M.R. Covey demonstrated in *The Speed of Trust: The One Thing That Changes Everything*, there are four aspects of trust: integrity, intent, competency, and results. Challenges come when one of these areas is lacking. If others challenge you about your schedule or any area of your life, assess these four areas, and you'll find that they have a lack of trust.

My client relationships and business commitments all hold mutual benefit, respect, and appreciation. I won't work with someone who demands that I sacrifice for their benefit. People who deserve me never ask me to sacrifice myself for them, and this includes family, friends, clients, business associates, and everyone else. Once you honor yourself and your own needs, it's magical how everyone else supports you to the same degree.

Create boundaries that are healthy for you within the framework of your time, schedule, and plans for each day. Take ownership of your day at home, in business, and with customers or clients. This allows you to show up day after day in power. You'll create unnecessary pain for yourself if you fail to establish enough space to breathe.

> Create boundaries that are healthy for you within the framework of your time, schedule, and plans for each day. Take ownership of your day at home, in business, and with customers or clients.

Executives who struggle with imposter syndrome might give up power over their schedule. This is a choice driven by feelings of inadequacy. You can control your day, your time, your schedule, and your actions. You can feel worthy of saying no. After that, it becomes easy to rebuild any credibility you lost while you neglected yourself and your schedule.

Ask for Help

An executive who's a results-generating machine can't focus on everything. When you try to handle everything, you'll focus on nothing. You deplete your ability to stay in your strengths, which diminishes optimal results.

It's important to find your sweet spot and live in it. To do this, you need allies, co-workers, and supporters who can handle the things outside of your zone of genius. When you offload and/or delegate these things, you'll allow someone else to be more efficient and effective in performing these tasks, which increases velocity and results.

The challenge that executives face is fearing a loss of control of what they delegate and the need for absolute certainty that the job has been completed and completed well. When you have a solid network of service providers and professionals who support you, you can establish trust within those relationships. Trust pays off when the need arises.

If you want to manage your time effectively, you have to relinquish control of the end-to-end creative process. You can maintain control of the vision, and you'll also have final approval of the end product, but the time between is a matter of trust. When you're able to trust others to execute within their zone of genius while you stay in your own, your results will be stronger, and you can focus where you have the most impact.

When I began my business, I focused on everything. When I needed a logo, I looked for software that would help me create a graphic. When I booked sales, I handled my accounting. When I needed a website, I learned some web design and designed myself a basic site. When I needed content for that website, I created, edited, and published it myself. When a client had an issue, I rushed into action to learn what I needed to learn so I could implement a solution for them.

For my first logo design, I found a website that offered graphics solutions. The site showed two fonts, and I selected the one I liked better. This process was repeated until the program honed in on my style preference. It then offered me six options for my logo. I chose one I liked and paid $30 to buy the rights to the file. It was all done in less than ten minutes, and I got a new logo for my first business. It wasn't perfect, but it was quick, good enough, and inexpensive.

When I needed a second set of logos, I wanted them to be designed by a professional.

"How much?" I asked Dale as we began the process to rebrand my business.

"$240," Dale said. "And Mike, I'm just getting started, and that's a friends and family discount."

"That's a lot for a logo!" I said. I was comparing this price to the $30 logo I'd created online.

We paused a second in our discussion as people sat down at the next booth in the busy cafe. People were settling in for dinner; it was more crowded than I expected.

"Wait a minute," Dale said. "I'm going to build a logo design that reflects your energy, intensity, and direct approach. We're going to put hours into the design. Once I get my business up and running, that same service will cost ten times that number."

I was still in the initial stages of my business and held on to a scarcity mindset. Even though I had plenty of cash reserves, I was afraid to spend money. But I knew I wanted to build something special, and what I saw in Dale's work captured my message and approach. I agreed to his price and asked if we could split up the payment—half up front and half after the design was complete. Dale agreed.

"We have a deal. When do we get started?"

Dale looked at me with a smile and said, "Right now. Tell me about your business and why you serve your clients."

I answered, "Executive business leaders hire me to help them feel as powerful and successful inside as they appear to those they lead. When I was in powerful positions, I felt alone and broken. Now I help leaders who are isolated and broken to feel their power."

Over the next few months, Dale learned my story and about my family's recovery. He learned my personality, approach to coaching, and values. He knew me better than I knew myself.

When I saw the design he'd created for the first time, I was shocked and astounded that Dale captured all of me inside a logo. I could see my essence, style, and approach. It was perfect.

"That's why I charge more than $30," Dale said. "Do you like it?"

"Very much!" I said.

"Will you do a testimonial for me and explain the difference between a web-designed logo and one from a branding special-ist?" he asked.

I smiled back at him and with an ear-to-ear grin replied, "I will."

As my clientele increased, I did as much as I could to reduce expenses. As the pace increased, the more things went unfinished or done half-assed. My accounting system and website were all poor quality. My results showed that, other than coaching and content creation, the rest of my research and execution was below average or average at best.

It's true that I maintained total control while I saved some money and kept it out of the hands of people whose time or service came at an expense. But the fact was that I cost myself even more business, success, and profitability because I had focused on things that didn't move the needle. When I speak or create content, I make money. When I do anything else, it impacts my business results.

At first, it was scary to hire a bookkeeper, marketing team, brand specialist, editor, and operations manager. All I could see were dollar signs and a loss of control over the finished product. I hired a bookkeeper, Jessie, first because I despise accounting related activities. But I soon experienced relief and freedom and felt the value of her support. I noticed an increase in my own results because of her work—and I was hooked.

I couldn't get rid of tasks fast enough.

"Jess, could you take over all invoicing for me?" I asked after we'd worked together for about six months. There were a few reasons why I hadn't given up the invoicing when she first took over my books: I enjoyed the invoicing process, I didn't have a process that I could hand off, and I didn't want to pay her more than the $125 per month she asked for (again, rock bottom prices for another start-up entrepreneur).

"Sure, Mike," Jessie replied. "Let's work on a process so I can take over in October."

"Thanks, Jess," I said, excited.

I'd dumped another responsibility. I still didn't have a process, but I knew her work, and I knew she was trustworthy, reliable, and that she performed at a high level.

"I can do that for $250 per month, including the bookkeeping work," she said.

"Done," I replied. "Let's set up a call for next week, and I'll walk you through what I've been doing so we can discuss a process," I said.

My biggest win came when I hired an operations manager. I posted two position descriptions on social media for what I called an administrative assistant. I was thinking small and inexpensive. I interviewed a few people but didn't find a good fit.

Tiffanie reached out to me and expressed interest in the administrative assistant role. I first dismissed the idea because she was overqualified. We discussed the job, and she told me that along with being a family coach and gifted pediatrician, her well-kept secret was that she loved web design, marketing, systems development, and project and program management.

That opened up my mind to new opportunities.

"I'll help take the administrative burdens off of your shoulders and free you up to coach and develop content. I'll make sure you stay in your lane," Tiffanie said in our first discussion.

"I'm not really comfortable with that," I said. "I'm not even sure if I feel worthy of that level of support," I replied.

"You deserve it, and it will also allow me to do what I love. I build systems that make things easier and perform administrative tasks," Tiffanie responded.

"Are you sure you want those big things and the smaller support elements, too?" I asked to confirm what I'd heard.

"It would be my pleasure, and we'll be a great team," Tiffanie said with complete confidence. The support that Tiffanie provided me more than paid her compensation. The amount of work that she took off of my shoulders created time and emotional freedom that was invaluable for my own quality of family time and connection.

Now I offload everything. I look for opportunities to seek support. I wrote this book, but I hired a book coach, Nancy Erickson, The Book Professor, to guide the process. The people I hire and subcontract are fulfilled when they get to provide backend support to see me shine. I allow them to exercise their genius, and I stay true to mine.

Trust and respect with your functional partners are required, and that's the most difficult challenge. When you develop trust and spend money to unload those things that aren't in your zone of genius, your results improve, and so do the results of what you hired out.

This discussion is relevant to executives too. The right support mechanisms help you stay focused and make an extreme impact on your effectiveness and results. You can get help with almost anything you can think of: a virtual assistant can keep you organized, there are dry-clean pick-up services, you can order your groceries online and have them delivered or hire a chef to prep your meals, and on and on. This may sound expensive and extravagant, but you must focus on your most critical tasks and allow others to do the same, so you can generate the best results for your life.

If you haven't established or developed the trust in your team that allows you to delegate without pause, work on building that trust or make adjustments so you can. If you're afraid of losing control of the result of their work or you feel the need to micromanage, then take a look at your fears and figure out why you hold them.

The imposter syndrome blinds leaders to what's important and urgent because all tasks appear equal in importance and urgency.

The imposter syndrome blinds leaders to what's important and urgent because all tasks appear equal in importance and urgency. Every task might feel like life or death and make you think you have to own everything. Let others contribute within their own zone of genius, and you'll create the exceptional results you desire.

Only Do What's Valuable

You'll probably find some inefficiencies and misallocated time in every day. I challenge you to write a list, and I bet you'll find some non-value-added activities. Go ahead. I dare you.

Maybe you don't have tons of wasted time, but I bet your efficiency isn't 100 percent, and I bet your time isn't always spent on the most important matters. There's wasted time in everyone's schedule. With that said, when you add up all the time you spend doing low priority tasks and compress it, I bet you'll find more time in your schedule.

I used to be guilty of activity for the sake of activity. But when I realized that I was preventing my own happiness, I found more time. I found time to regroup, recharge, unwind, and recover. Everyone gets the same twenty-four hours in a day. Successful people who also enjoy their life use their twenty-four hours more effectively and efficiently.

I thought I was busy, and I was, but I was busy doing unnecessary things. I could have eliminated, delegated, or delayed most activities and focused on the critical ones. I never took the time to manage my day, especially in corporate jobs.

When I was with Danaher Corporation, we went through a major downsizing after a merger and a stock market slide. We used a process called *empty chair kaizen* to manage the reorganization. The process of kaizen is to make better, and empty chair kaizen was "to make the organization better" when a seat was left open.

"Okay, fellas," my boss, Brad, said as he stood in front of an empty whiteboard with a marker. "What were Robert's responsibilities? I want everything. Leave nothing out."

"He managed the television team," Nathan said.

"His projects are on the team project plan," said Jack.

"He led the production walk once a week," I said.

All the managers in the room, the six of us that were left, and Brad, our boss, continued to list the twenty-five to thirty responsibilities that Robert carried out.

"Awesome. That's a lot of tasks," Brad said, surprised as the rest of us that Robert had carried so much. But every one of us had that much on our plates, and we knew what was coming next.

"What on this list can we eliminate or make more manageable?" Brad asked.

"We can stop the weekly report and move to monthly reports," Rick suggested.

"Done," Brad agreed.

"We can review the project list and eliminate all of the nice-to-haves that aren't critical," Allen said.

"Let's do that today, too," Brad said. "Anything else?"

"That's all I can see," I said.

"So, how will we divide up his team and share in daily management?" Brad asked.

We went through the list and reassigned or eliminated every task on the list. We also negotiated a bit with our boss and off-loaded or eliminated some of our own tasks to make room for the newly assigned tasks and responsibilities. After everything on the list was reassigned and we all agreed that the delegation was manageable, we raised our hands in a show of agreement.

We did this same process four more times as our team of seven shrank to two. In the end, Rick and I were the only two managers left within depot operations, and we only had the most critical responsibilities and authorities. When we started the process, I thought it was impossible to manage our service depot operations with only two managers when we used to have seven, but the process revealed that there are non-value-added activities that every person, team, or organization does that can be eliminated without a loss of performance.

So look at the details of your day. You'll find opportunities to capture more time. List everything you do and create a scale that helps you understand what value each task plays in your life to drive health, wealth, and love. Use the urgency and importance matrix in Stephen R. Covey's *The 7 Habits of Highly Effective People*. Make a four-block diagram with urgency on one axis and importance on the other. The goal is to only work on tasks that are important but not urgent. Covey advises to get to the root issue and solve the process breakdown that caused any task to become urgent and important. Next, determine if tasks that are urgent and not important are required. Ignore tasks that are not important and not urgent. Focus future efforts and attention only on creating processes which drive focus to the important but not urgent block.

When you identify your daily focus activities, you'll be surprised at how much time you can free to shift your day toward increased health, wealth, and love. Make the changes little by little.

My day is now is a blend of professional expansion and enjoying my existence. My wife and I have built a home-based business, and we've created an integrated work-life experience. I choose to do only the things that I value. We don't turn on the television unless we know we're going to watch a specific show or movie, and that time is finite. We use this time to connect and relate, not to sedate or pass the time. We don't fill our day with activities for the sake of activities. We're more than comfortable and happy to sit and talk. We're careful to watch what we allow into our lives, and because of that, we have plenty of time for business and relationship development.

We were taught as children that life is difficult and chaotic. We proved time and time again that this is a false belief. There are people who are more financially well-off, but I guarantee there's no one with the combination of financial freedom and love that we enjoy. This all began when we eliminated things from our lives that didn't serve us.

Executive leaders who feel imposter syndrome overload themselves with unnecessary activities. Because of the feeling of overwhelm, every activity you touch feels critical, and you can't discern between critical and non-critical activity. If you take a step back, seek an outside source, and review all of the tasks you touch, you can rearrange the tasks and your day to create more powerful results. Over time, you gave up your power, and you can take back that power decision by decision and activity by activity.

Executive leaders who feel imposter syndrome overload themselves with unnecessary activities. Because of the feeling of overwhelm, every activity you touch feels critical, and you can't discern between critical and non-critical activity.

Busyness Out of Fear

"I feel like I should be doing something else," Tony Fonte said after he completed his daily routine of physical, mental, and emotional exercises, as well his activities that generated most of his new business.

"Why?" I asked.

"Because I've always stayed busy," he replied.

"Did your busyness get results?" I questioned.

"No."

I paused and allowed him to let that anchor a bit. "Then why do the thing if it doesn't generate results?" I asked.

"I guess it's because I thought I needed to stay busy. I've always thought that people who weren't busy were lazy," he said.

"And you don't want to be considered lazy."

"I don't," he said.

"Who taught you that inactivity was lazy?"

"My dad, I guess," he replied.

"Was your dad busy?" I asked.

"Always," he said.

"Did he make time for you?"

"Not really," he said.

"Do you wish he had?" I dug deeper.

"I do. That's why I want to spend more time with Kailee (his thirteen-year-old daughter)."

"Perfect," I said. "You wish your dad had spent more time with you, you've finished all your most critical work that will create results, and now you feel lazy for not doing more. Even some guilt and shame?" I questioned.

"Yes," he said.

"Let me get this straight again. You're finished all of the tasks that we agreed will move the needle, you have free time on your hands, Kailee is home, but instead of spending more time with Kailee, like you wanted your dad to spend with you, you feel guilty and shameful and look for non-value-added activity to do instead of spending time with your daughter. Am I getting this right?" I said, almost out of breath.

"I see your point," Tony confessed.

"When your dad finished all of the important work he needed to accomplish, what if he'd found a bunch of garbage work to fill the time. How would you feel?" I continued.

Tears welled up in Tony's eyes. "He did that all the time," he said. His shoulders slumped.

"How did that make you feel?" I asked.

"Like I didn't matter. Like I mattered less than the garbage stuff he did instead of spending time with me," he said almost in a whisper.

"Are you operating like your dad to prove to that little boy that you're not garbage, to find justification in what your dad did?" I asked.

With more tears in his eyes, he said, "And I've neglected Kailee because busyness means that I'm not lazy, I don't want to be lazy, and she feels like she matters less than the meaningless stuff I'm doing," he replied.

"Are all of the critical tasks done, Tony?" I asked, to bring the conversation full circle.

"Yes," he said.

"Then go spend time with your daughter, brother. Go make her feel special. Treat her the way you wanted to be treated. Do your most important tasks that will keep her safe and secure, then give her your time and attention. No guilt. No shame," I said with emphasis.

"Thanks, Mike," Tony said.

"Anytime, brother."

———

I work with many professionals who keep themselves busy. Some remain productive for the sake of productivity, focusing on value-added activity that will move the needle. I find that those who focus only on productive, value-add activity are exceptions and rare. Often, I find professional's busyness has more to do with their survival than to add value. Their activity is work for the sake of work more than for effectiveness. Most feel that if they aren't active and busy, then they don't add enough value. Their busyness comes from inadequacy and insecurity.

Everyone has a certain amount of inadequacy and insecurity. These feelings can cause paralysis and inactivity, but feelings of inadequacy and insecurity can also drive exceptional performance, accomplishment, and results. People who feel insecure and inadequate often pursue additional education, read to expand their knowledge, exercise to increase their health, and push for increased results. They are healthy habits to create as long as they don't consume you.

Professionals press ahead and hope to overcome the feelings of inadequacy and insecurity, but if you reframe these as conditions that serve a productive purpose, you can appreciate them as internal drivers forward that can help free you from the pressure of constant busyness for the sake of feeling adequate and secure. You'll find freedom *within* your inadequacy and insecurity, not freedom *from* your inadequacy and insecurity. Consider that when you felt adequate and secure, you could have packed it in and stayed home to eat bonbons and binge-watch shows.

Busyness for the sake of busyness is never the answer. If your activity doesn't help you move the needle, achieve your goals, achieve compliance, or expand your circumstances, the activity isn't worthwhile.

Busyness for the sake of busyness is never the answer. If your activity doesn't help you move the needle, achieve your goals, achieve compliance, or expand your circumstances, the activity isn't worthwhile. When you're caught up in an insanity loop of your feelings, emotions, inadequacy, or insecurity to the degree that it causes constant unproductive activity, it's time to take inventory and gain new awareness to free up some time and relax.

Stacy is an executive with a Fortune 75 aerospace company. We began working together in February of 2018. She hired me because she'd been passed over for promotions multiple times, and she knew she had some blind spots to identify and address.

Stacy was a busy person. She was successful in her career and outworked everyone. She hustled every day. She worked a lot and kept busy in her work life, personal life, and even in her relationships. She needed to be active for the sake of being active. She never took the time to relax.

She mentioned that even when she went on vacation, she planned an aggressive agenda that drove everyone crazy as they hustled from one activity to another while Stacy drove the agenda. She admitted that she loved the idea of finding relaxation and rest in stillness. She also admitted that most of her activity was just busyness with no value-add.

"You like to stay busy?" I asked Stacy on our video call.

"I do. I love to fill my schedule up, but sometimes I can't even breathe," she said.

"Why?" I dug.

"I don't know," she replied in an honest and sincere tone.

"Why are you afraid of sitting still?" I asked.

"Never thought about that. Because I get bored probably," she replied.

"Are you afraid of your thoughts?" I dug deeper.

"Maybe," she said.

"Does busyness keep you from your thoughts and help you to avoid feeling what you don't want to feel?" I asked.

"Maybe," she said again.

"Tell me about your childhood, when you were ten years old and younger," I requested.

"I don't want to talk about my childhood," Stacy snapped back.

"Which is precisely why we should talk about your childhood, Stacy."

"What's that going to help?" she asked.

"I won't know until I learn more," I answered.

"My mom was always gone, and I was afraid, so I kept myself busy and took care of my brothers," she said, her voice cracking with emotion in every word.

"Tell me more," I said. I knew that this was a breakthrough.

We dug into her life history and discovered many events in her past—in her childhood—that imprisoned her in a constant state of insecurity. No amount of money, no job title, validation, or possession could soothe the insecurity she'd developed from her traumas. Her busyness was a means to overcome her fears and insecurities.

In one session, when we dug deep, she cried and restated, "I don't want to talk about my childhood." I again explained that her childhood traumas drove her fears and her behavior. With reluctance, she agreed to proceed.

Past traumas are difficult to explore, but awareness of them is the greatest path to healing. When we discuss and release the trauma, which includes forgiving ourselves and others, we can release the poisonous energy that's been stuck in our bodies since the event occurred.

As we discussed each traumatic memory in her life, the reason for Stacy's busyness became clear. She'd been left alone to fend for herself and her siblings well before she was a teenager. Her single mother worked, and the burden of the home responsibilities was on Stacy's shoulders. She was afraid for the well-being of her younger siblings, who relied on her for everything. This young girl was their mother. That same burden of responsibility and busyness had been branded on Stacy's subconscious, and she was still living out those traumas in adulthood.

The sessions were painful, and we did a lot of shadow work, but with each new discovery, Stacy felt a deeper sense of awareness. That same busyness had created massive results in her life. However, it had caused a plateau in her career, and gaining new confidence, courage, and clarity helped her reach the next level.

We continued to dive into what drove her insecurity and pulled emotional weed after emotional weed. We brought new awareness forward into her current behavior and circumstances, and Stacy saw that she approached her life and responsibilities from a place of fear. As we eliminated her baseline fears from previous experiences, she became more comfortable and confident in her own skin.

About six months into our coaching relationship, Stacy slowed her busyness, demonstrated more confidence, courage, and clarity, and was promoted to her current executive position. In this position, she's responsible for offices and departments across the globe. She's a powerful leader, and she's well prepared, open to feedback, and able to put plans into swift action.

Stacy had, at first, run from pain, but now she runs toward purpose and performance. She's gained confidence that her feet are planted underneath her. She realizes that excessive preparation and busyness, once done out of fear, now drive her performance. She's a high-powered leader who focuses on value-add activity instead of activity for the sake of activity.

Stacy sends me pictures from her poolside or on vacation. She takes the time to brag to me about how she craves solitude, inactivity, and calm. She expresses that when she recharges, she gains higher levels of focus and concentration for when she's involved in productive activity. She now has the confidence to stand up to her peers, leaders, and others.

The reason for her professional plateau was that she faced her role and responsibilities from a place of fear and insecurity. When she shifted her busyness to intense focus on value-added activity, her performance soared, and people took immediate notice.

It's important to understand whether your activity is driven by fear or driven by passion for your goals. Fear means that you'll never feel safe, and you won't find fulfillment in activities from that perspective. You're counting on the goal to provide fulfillment, but the mind and body want to *want* more than they want to *have* more. When you run toward passion and purpose, you are fulfilled by the activity, not the goals. Drive and accomplishment based on passion for the pursuit of goals or a vision creates energy, excitement, and allows some pockets for recovery, rest, and relaxation. Imposters in charge who are living in a state of fear are a ticking

> **Imposters in charge who are living in a state of fear are a ticking time bomb. With awareness and by modifying your behaviors, you can shift from fear to passion.**

time bomb. With awareness and by modifying your behaviors, you can shift from fear to passion.

Relax

Sometimes, professionals don't feel worthy of a pause, and they struggle to take time to decompress. They feel a need to sacrifice themselves for their missions, organizations, or teams. This is appropriate for first responders and the military, but there's no reasonable cause to sacrifice your welfare in the corporate world. We know that because your organization will replace you within minutes of your separation.

I practiced self-sacrifice in every role I held, which was an attitude I learned in the United States Marine Corps and carried into the corporate world. But the honor, dignity, and respect you feel in the corporate world don't warrant that level of commitment. I only practiced extreme self-sacrifice in corporate America because I felt unworthy.

My time as second-in-command at SunCoke Energy was a prime example. When I accepted the position, I got a significant compensation bump, as well as a responsibility and authority bump.

The associates in our plant were hard workers. They worked long hours. I saw a lot of tired, exhausted guys and gals; that was the culture. Everyone justified the hours worked because of the great pay and benefits. People who shoveled coal made more than $70,000 per year. They sacrificed to do their job, but they also knew when to call it quits and get some rest. Overall, they pushed themselves and worked hard, and they played hard, too.

I didn't. I worked hard. That was it.

I pulled into the parking lot on a Sunday morning with a few boxes of donuts. Since the plant was a 24/7, 365-days-a-year operation, our supervisors and team members were at the plant at all hours to manage the ovens. We injected metallurgical coal into the 2,000-degree ovens, and forty-eight hours later, extracted metallurgical coke. The smell of baking coal and a glow of fire around the doors were constant.

"What are you doing here?" Tom, a machine supervisor, asked.

"Bringing the guy some donuts," I replied.

"Mike, we were on the phone yesterday afternoon about the plant. Give it a break, man. I've got it. Go home and spend time with your family. You've got a long week ahead of you," he reassured me.

Tom was my most senior machine supervisor, and he ran a crew of five machine operators. He was the senior person in the plant on the weekends. He was seasoned and knowledgeable, and he knew how to run the plant.

"Thanks, Tom, but I want to show my appreciation for your sacrifice on the weekends, the sacrifice of your family and friends," I said.

"Mike, it's *my shift*. I'm taken care of. I've been off all week. You've been here all week, and now you won't disconnect," he replied.

"I appreciate you, Tom. I feel bad about letting down while you guys are working," I said.

"There's always someone here, Mike, so you better find a way to relax and disconnect," he said.

"I'll disconnect after I'm dead," I said with pride and exhaustion in my voice. "Go get the guys so they can have a donut."

———

I put in twelve to sixteen hours days and worked from the time I got up until the time I went to bed. I made impromptu visits to the plant on the weekends, checked the status of the operation seven days per week, called the supervisors on each shift, and gave more than was expected. I forced myself to become exhausted before I shut down.

My boss reminded me to slow down and balance my life and schedule. For some reason, I felt that sacrifice—even sacrificing my own health and happiness—was what I deserved for the income level I received. I doubted the value of my own contribution, so I made up for that up by being overly involved. I was ever-present in the plant, online, and over the phone because I felt I had to prove my worth.

Over twenty months, I ran myself ragged. My marriage suffered, my health suffered, my relationships with my children suffered, and the folks at the plant saw me as a micromanager. It was all non-value-added activity. I spent a lot of time connected to the plant but made no significant contribution because I was exhausted and depleted.

That's when my downfall began. I felt such little self-worth that I struggled to justify the massive income and benefits I received. I chased feelings of worth, and even though I made sacrifice after sacrifice, I never felt that I ever gave equal value for value.

When I was terminated twenty months into that position, it was almost a relief because I no longer had to justify the burden of that large salary. My self-worth took another hit when I was fired, but at least I didn't think of a big number every time I tried to sleep.

———

When I began my journey of self-mastery, I had deep-seated issues about my self-worth and self-value. I carried the burden of a large income while feeling unworthy overall. That feeling lingered over me like a dark cloud.

So I reframed my worth and value in a new context—my humanity. My worth and value are now derived simply from my existence, not from a level of education, title, position, salary, or any other factor outside of myself. I derive worth and value as part of my birthright. The fact that I breathe makes me worthy, and I never need to justify, confirm, prove, or gain approval for that. I treat each person as I treat myself: worthy of everything they're willing to achieve.

There's time for work and time for rest. Rest and relaxation enable performance, and the two must be separated to maintain and function at the level expected in the executive ranks. Executive leaders are compensated based on impact they have and the experience they possess. Executive level compensation is adjusted based on the value provided, not the amount you sacrifice your own health and relationships. There's plenty of time in a day and week to relax. Time off is required to maintain adequate fuel in the tank to produce results.

A leader who suffers from imposter syndrome will often feel that relaxation time will reduce their overall value and performance. This false belief is derived because of a lack of appreciation for yourself. You deserve a quality of life greater than your compensation. Compensation does not justify sacrifice. Leaders under the spell of imposter syndrome must take back the power they have given up and remember their true value.

It's insane to believe that you're being rewarded for how willing you are to kill yourself for the good of a corporate organization. You're much more valuable than a financial or business objective. Relax into your true nature, value, and worth. Feel your true power within. Your superpowers—your confidence, courage, clarity of purpose, happiness, joy, peace, fulfillment, satisfaction, and many other exciting destinations—have been hiding in places where you haven't looked. They've been there all along—inside of you—waiting for

> **Everything you want is inside of you. What's inside of you is the only thing that really matters.**

you to discover them. They've been there all along; you were just looking in all the wrong places this whole time. Everything you want is inside of you. What's inside of you is the only thing that really matters.

Chapter 7 Work

Are You Showing Up For Yourself?

1. Do you feel that your worth and value are wrapped up in your busyness?

2. Are you unable to ask for help or get support when you feel overwhelmed?

3. Do you prioritize based on the urgency and importance of tasks? When you ignore a task that isn't urgent or important, do you feel confident in your decision?

4. Do you relax? Do you take time to recharge? Do you take time off?

Try This!

1. Read or reread the chapter titled "Putting First Things First" in Stephen R. Covey's *The 7 Habits of Highly Effective People*. Plot your entire day. Eliminate, manage, delegate, and execute the tasks according to Covey's recommendations. This will help you create time and space in your day.

2. If you're a chronic workaholic, plan a vacation, and ask your peers to hold you accountable to be fully present during your time away—no work, no cellphones, no laptop, no connecting. Disconnect and see that the organization runs in your absence. You'll be just as valuable when you return as when you leave, even more, because you're recharged.

3. Create a daily schedule that works in your best interests to keep you focused, present, and effective. Share this schedule with others, seek their support, and ask for accountability. You'll find that the right people will celebrate you for taking ownership of your performance.

Connection.

If the teacher is not connecting you to yourself...

If you are being guided to seek attainment, relationships, wealth, identity, or health as a source of status, happiness, or self-worth...

They're teaching you to find more chaos and dis-ease in your life.

Things outside of you are fun, exciting, and desirable, certainly.

You were born to create, achieve, and build.

Evolution requires creation.

Not for the sake of happiness....

But for the sake of realizing how powerful you are.

You can create anything you want.

But your true power, happiness, and identity lie within.

Once you connect to your inner power...

You'll no longer view external power as the destination.

The destination is hidden within your power that sleeps.

When that awakens, you'll finally see that more is not better.

More is not security.

More does not create happiness.

Happiness and excitement are different.

Happiness is eternal.

Excitement and fun have a half-life.

Creating and building are exciting and fun.

But the power within is eternal and is all you truly require.

Everything else is just a means to discover what's hidden inside.

And you can't find that outside of yourself.

CHAPTER 8
FROM IMPOSTER TO MISFIT.

We're nearing the end of this journey, and I hope you see the connection between rejecting yourself—your desires, your physical, mental, and emotional well-being, your vision, your worth, and everything else about you—and the imposter syndrome. Look no further than full, absolute, unconditional, infinite acceptance of all that you are, even your darkness, to find the happiness, peace, love, and joy you seek. You've rejected everything about yourself, and it hasn't worked. How has rejecting yourself brought you to purpose?

From the second you were born, you've grasped for acceptance. You looked for ways to please your parents, teachers, friends, partners, children, boss, employees, and anyone else you came into contact with. You overextended yourself for everyone else's benefit. That's caused you extreme chaos and suffering. Maybe you overextended yourself so much that you've now put up barriers so thick that they push everyone else away, all because you don't trust yourself.

This book found you, and you finished reading it because there's some inner work that you're being guided to perform. Nothing outside of you requires change. What needs to be changed is how you accept, trust, appreciate, love, and relate with yourself. When you finally understand that self-acceptance and surrender to your design and everything about you is the way to freedom, you'll finally see the chaos you've lived in your entire life.

That is your work. Discover yourself. Be yourself. Be. That's all this life is about—realizing who you are, and in the process, realizing who you are not.

I propose a new concept for you. You might feel like an imposter in one or more areas of life. Dive inside. Understand what you are rejecting about yourself in that area or areas of life. Why do you feel you can't fully show up? Why do you feel incomplete? Why do you think that just being you will bring about failure? Who taught you that you aren't enough? What events convinced you that you must reject yourself as you are designed? Work from there. You don't need to correct anything else. You'll discover all the answers you're seeking are in those questions. The external shift will unfold naturally.

I am committed to you. If you don't trust yourself, borrow my trust until you can trust yourself. If you aren't confident in yourself, borrow my confidence for a while. In the process, the artificial life you've built might begin to dismantle. And just like the life I've created, as the old fake life crumbles, a new aligned life will be rebuilt from the ashes.

I once felt like an imposter. The Imposter in Charge. I looked for evidence for why I wasn't good enough. And I found it everywhere. That was self-rejection. Self-rejection and suffering never create happiness, love, peace, and joy—only more self-rejection and suffering. Embracing yourself and accepting yourself, wherever you are, is the springboard to everything you seek.

Before we part ways, I make one final proposal. I'd like you to reframe the word *imposter*. Instead, let's use the word *misfit*. There are 7.7 billion people on the planet, and no two of us are alike. When you feel like an imposter, it's because you don't feel like everyone else. You've been trying to force yourself into a box that appears to fit everyone else—as if we were all designed the same!

You were designed to be unique. You aren't different; we all have skin, cells, organs, and similar human features, but the characters we play are unique. It's natural to have unique perspectives, talents, likes and dislikes, and everything else. You aren't broken, and you don't need to be fixed. You may be playing a character that you designed, and that might, indeed, have created the imposter syndrome, but you are not an imposter. You are very real.

We are ALL misfits. We are misfits because of the unique value we bring to this human experience. Life teaches us to fall in line and sleep with the masses of humanity. Misfits define success authentically and individually according to our own inner compass. Embrace your inner misfit. Your misfit nature is what creates the value you bring to the world.

As you learn to trust, embrace, and accept who you are in this human lifetime, I'll leave you with this:

- You have a human body that will die and fall to ash.

- You have a human mind which will cease to process thought.

- You ARE an infinite, eternal, powerful, and abundant soul.

And we share one awareness, one consciousness. But you are a misfit, just like the rest of us. And we all share one soul.

You are not an imposter. You are The Misfit Soul.

In the Hole.

Yesterday, I was blessed with the opportunity to meet
with my newest client for the first time.

He's a good guy.

He's like many of us.

He's my old self.

My client lacks basic self-confidence, and this lack of
confidence trickles into every area of his life.

These issues caused some pain in the personal and
professional parts of his life.

The issues took a toll on his health.

We began some basic work of rebuilding. Together, we
built some basic awareness and tools around his daily
habits to reclaim his self-care and personal power.

At work, some folks run over him because he's allowed them
to treat him like he feels, less valuable than others.

We put basic building blocks in place to rediscover his
true worthiness and incredible presence on earth.

He's a good guy.

He'll soon begin to feel the amazing creation that he is.
It's a matter of time and some work.

There's nothing in the world that satisfies me more than
helping others see past their own blind-spots.

I see small successes in my clients, and I'm reminded of
how much I value my new life, a work life that is my
personal life, and a personal life that is my work.

I live life to help others avoid traps into which I have
fallen victim in the past.

There was no one to help me avoid them, so I found the traps.

Only after I became trapped did I seek support. And I
found it.

My coach saved my life.

I like to feel that I save lives, too. At a minimum, I assist
others in avoiding rock bottom.

I found my rock bottom. It hurt.

I'm reminded of a story:

A man was trapped in a deep hole in the middle of a busy urban street.

People walked by him as he screamed for help.

"Hey! I need help! I'm trapped in this hole!"

People saw him in the hole and continued about their day. They pondered their own problems.

After many screams, a pastor stopped and spoke to the man. "What do you need, my son?" asked the pastor.

"I'm trapped in this hole! Can you help me?"

The pastor offered a prayer and went about his day.

After a few more screams, a psychiatrist stopped and asked what was wrong.

"I'm trapped in this hole! Can you help me?"

The psychiatrist threw a bottle of pills in the hole and went about his day.

After a few more screams, a therapist stopped and inquired about the situation.

"I'm trapped in this hole! Can you help me?"

The therapist listened intently, offered some encouragement, offered to schedule another session, and went about her day.

Later that day, after many people walked by, and the man was losing his voice, a coach heard his screams and went to see what was happening.

"I'm trapped in this hole! Can you help me?"

The man went on to explain that he had been in the hole all day and was worried that he'd never get out of the hole.

He asked for and received help, but he was still in the hole and was losing hope.

The coach jumped in the hole with the man.

The man was confused and expressed surprise that the coach had jumped in the hole and now they were both stuck.

The man's hopelessness increased.

THE IMPOSTER IN CHARGE.

With confidence, the coach expressed, "I jumped in because
    I've been in this exact hole and was once trapped. I
    know the way out and can show you how to get out.
    Follow me."
And they both made their way out of the hole.

My story is one of pain and suffering of low self-worth,
    low self-value, low self-esteem, zero happiness inside,
    and a lifetime of trying to find happiness on the
    outside that was never available.
There was never happiness on the inside.
There was alcoholism, termination from executive
    positions, potential divorce, addiction, physical,
    mental, emotional, sexual abuse...
I found my way out of the hole with the help of a coach.
Now, I show others the way out.
I love my new life. I help others love theirs as well.
And I'm rewarded regularly with a new client
    conversation that starts with both of us in a hole. And
    my journey is the most rewarding experience I've
    ever experienced.
I can show you the way out of the hole.
I know the way.
Are you ready?

ABOUT THE AUTHOR

Mike Kitko is a former executive leader, a Marine veteran, and a former failure. He was raised to feel he like was never good enough, never enough to matter, and never enough to succeed. The chase for validation and a feeling of "success" led him to become an alcoholic and suicidal, and he was physically, mentally, and emotionally abusive to his family—even sexually abusive to his wife. He spent close to twenty years in corporate America, most of that time feeling like an imposter or a fake, even though all the external signs of success were present—big house, nice cars, lots of savings, and vacations. His insides eroded more and more every day until he ultimately collapsed personally and professionally.

With a single, momentary decision, his entire life turned around, including his health, his family, his success, and the way he shows up in the world. Mike stopped being The Imposter In Charge and went on a journey of self-discovery that has led to a total transformation and reinvention. That journey continues today.

CPSIA information can be obtained
at www.ICGtesting.com
Printed in the USA
LVHW081106141019
634116LV00018B/442/P